Make It Quick

PLASTIC CANVAS ™

the Needlecraft® Shop

CONTENTS

CHAPTER FIVE

QUICK HOLIDAY FUN

CHAPTER FOUR

FAST FAMILY FAVORITES

Product Development Director ANDY ASHLEY
Publishing Services Director ANGE VAN ARMAN
Plastic Canvas Design Manager FRAN ROHUS
Product Development Staff MICKIE AKINS
DARLA HASSELL
SANDRA MILLER MAXFIELD
ALICE MITCHELL
ELIZABETH ANN WHITE
Senior Editor JUDY CROW
Editor KRIS KIRST
Associate Editors JAIMIE DAVENPORT
SHIRLEY PATRICK
Book Design GREG SMITH
Graphic Artist GLENDA CHAMBERLAIN
Photographers SCOTT CAMPBELL
ANDY J. BURNFIELD
Photo Stylist MARTHA COQUAT

Chief Executive Officer JOHN ROBINSON
Marketing Director SCOTT MOSS

Customer Service 1-800-449-0440
Pattern Services (903) 636-5140

CREDITS
Sincerest thanks to all the designers,
manufacturers and other professionals
whose dedication has made this book possible.

Special thanks to
Quebecor Printing Book Group, Kingsport, Tennessee

Library of Congress Cataloging-in-Publication Data
ISBN: 1-57367-115-0
First Printing: 2001
Library of Congress Catalog Card Number: 2001130064
Published and Distributed by
The Needlecraft Shop, Big Sandy, Texas 75755
Printed in the United States of America.

Visit us at **NeedlecraftShop.com**

DEAR FRIENDS,

*I make a daily effort to create a comfortable
and safe home environment for my family. I
want it to be the type of home that is a haven,
a type of sanctuary, a place we can discard
the burdens of the day and rejuvenate.*

*I don't think this is an unusual feeling.
Most mothers feel this way. When I was a
child living at home, my mother created this
same type of home environment. She would
add small touches like fresh flowers, sweetly
scented candles and always, always
kept the home tidy.*

*The times have changed. As mothers we still
have the same desires, but we don't have the
same schedules. I so often feel short changed.
Not only do I not keep up with my household
duties the way I prefer, I don't seem to have
much time to nurture my creative spirit.*

*When the thought came to me to pull
together a collection of quick-to-stitch plastic
canvas projects, it seemed as though a large
burden unloaded from me. This is the type of
book I could really use. I won't have to spend
time thumbing through numerous magazines
and books looking for the quick projects. They
are all right here, in one place. With the
small amount of time I have for enjoying my
love of plastic canvas, having this book is a
welcomed solution.*

*I hope this book is as refreshing to you, too.
With a little more time for me, I'm sure my
family and home will be that much more cozy
and comfortable.*

Many happy stitches,

Fran Rohus

Chapter One
SNAPPY
KITCHEN FIXIN'S

CHEF POCKET

*Every cook can use a helping hand in the kitchen,
and this handsome chef is just the one to lend assistance.*

SIZE
10" x 23¼" [25.4cm x 59.1cm].

SKILL LEVEL: Average

MATERIALS
- 4½ sheets of 7-mesh plastic canvas
- 2" [5.1cm] sawtooth hanger
- Craft glue or glue gun
- Worsted-weight or plastic canvas yarn; for amounts see Color Key.

CUTTING INSTRUCTIONS
A: For Body Front and Backing, cut two (one for Front and one for Backing) 61w x 90h-holes (no graph).

B: For Head Front and Backing, cut two (one for Front and one for Backing) according to graph.

C: For Feet Front and Backing, cut two (one for Front and one for Backing) according to graph.

D: For Hat Front and Backing, cut two (one for Front and one for Backing) according to graph.

E: For Mustache, cut one according to graph.

F: For Nose, cut one according to graph.

G: For Tie, cut one according to graph.

H: For Pocket, cut one 48w x 36h-holes (no graph).

STITCHING INSTRUCTIONS
NOTE: One of each A-D pieces are not worked for Backings.

1: Using colors and stitches indicated, work one B, one C, one D and E-G pieces according to graphs; work one A for Front according to Body Stitch Pattern Guide. Fill in uncoded area of D and work H using white and continental stitch. With matching colors, overcast edges of E-H pieces.

2: Using black and embroidery stitches indicated (Leave 1½" [3.8cm] loops on modified turkey work stitches.) embroider detail on Front B as indicated on graph.

3: Holding one Backing A-D piece to wrong side of each corresponding Front, with matching colors, whipstitch together.

4: Glue Mustache and Nose to right side of Head as indicated; glue Hat to Head as shown in photo. Glue Feet and sawtooth hanger to Body back and Head and Pocket sides and bottom to Body as shown in photo.

—*Designed by Trudy Bath Smith*

COLOR KEY: Chef Pocket

Worsted-weight	YARN AMOUNT
☐ White	3 oz. [85.1g]
☐ Flesh Tone	15 yds. [13.7m]
■ Black	12 yds. [11m]
■ Christmas Red	5 yds. [4.6m]
■ Gray	2 yds. [1.8m]

STITCH KEY:
- ⦿ French Knot
- ⧖ Modified Turkey Work

PLACEMENTS:
- ☐ Nose
- ☐ Mustache

G – Tie
(19w x 30h-hole piece)
Cut 1 & work.

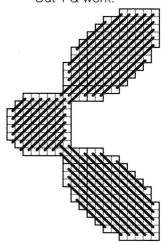

F – Nose
(6w x 5h-hole piece)
Cut 1 & work.

B – Head Front & Backing
(51w x 31h-hole pieces) Cut 2.
Work 1 for Front & leave 1 unworked for Backing.

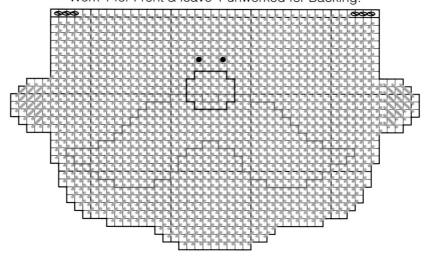

Body Stitch Pattern Guide
Continue established pattern across entire piece.

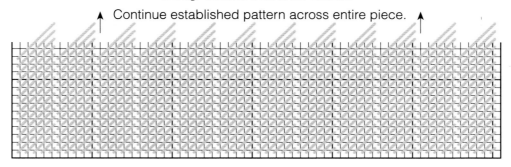

E – Mustache
(36w x 12h-hole piece) Cut 1 & work.

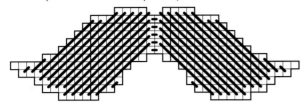

COLOR KEY: Chef Pocket

Worsted-weight		YARN AMOUNT
☐ White	3 oz.	[85.1g]
☐ Flesh Tone	15 yds.	[13.7m]
■ Black	12 yds.	[11m]
■ Christmas Red	5 yds.	[4.6m]
☐ Gray	2 yds.	[1.8m]

STITCH KEY:

⊙ French Knot
⊠ Modified Turkey Work

PLACEMENTS:

☐ Nose
☐ Mustache

C – Feet Front & Backing
(51w x 15h-hole pieces) Cut 2.
Work 1 for Front & leave 1 unworked for Backing.

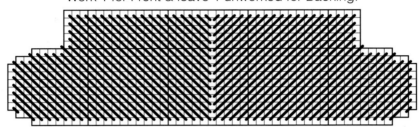

D – Hat Front & Backing
(60w x 38h-hole pieces) Cut 2.
Work 1 for Front & leave 1 unworked for Backing.

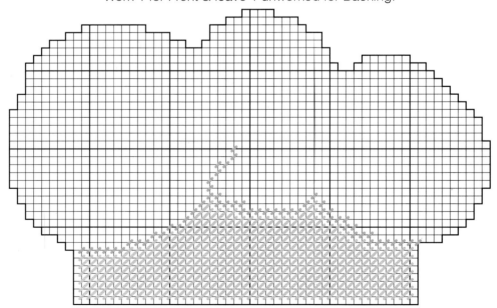

Celebration Coasters

Perk up any party with these seasonal and sensible coaster sensations.

SPOOKY COASTERS

SIZES
Each Coaster is 4⅝" x 4½" [11.7cm x 11.4cm]; Holder is 1¾" x 5¾" x 3⅝" tall [4.4cm x 14.6cm x 9.2cm].

SKILL LEVEL: Average

MATERIALS
- 1¼ sheets of 7-mesh plastic canvas
- No. 3 pearl cotton or six-strand embroidery floss; for amounts see Color Key.
- Worsted-weight or plastic canvas yarn; for amounts see Color Key.

CUTTING INSTRUCTIONS
A: For Coasters, cut four according to graph.
B: For Holder Front, cut one according to graph.
C: For Holder Back, cut one 33w x 11h-holes.
D: For Holder Sides, cut two 10w x 11h-holes.

E: For Holder Bottom, cut one 33w x 10h-holes.

STITCHING INSTRUCTIONS
1: Using colors and stitches indicated, work pieces according to graphs; fill in uncoded areas of A pieces using white and continental stitch. With indicated and matching colors, overcast edges of A pieces.

2: Using pearl cotton or six strands floss and embroidery stitches indicated, embroider detail on A and B pieces as indicated on graphs.

3: With black yarn, whipstitch B-E pieces together as indicated and according to Holder Assembly Illustration; overcast unfinished edges.

—Designed by Michele Wilcox

A – Coaster
(30w x 29h-hole pieces) Cut 4 & work.

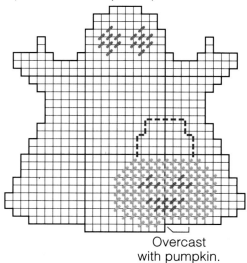

Overcast
with pumpkin.

C – Holder Back
(33w x 11h-hole piece) Cut 1 & work.

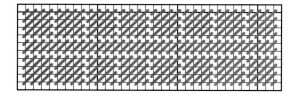

E – Holder Bottom
(33w x 10h-hole piece) Cut 1 & work.

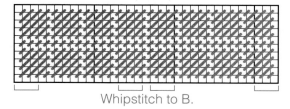

Whipstitch to B.

B – Holder Front
(37w x 23h-hole piece) Cut 1 & work.

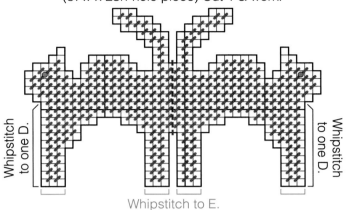

Whipstitch to one D.

Whipstitch to one D.

Whipstitch to E.

D – Holder Side
(10w x 11h-hole pieces)
Cut 2 & work.

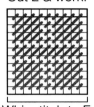

Whipstitch to E.

COLOR KEY: Spooky Coasters

No. 3 pearl cotton or floss	AMOUNT
■ Black	2 yds. [1.8m]
■ Beige	1/2 yd. [0.5m]
■ Green	1/2 yd. [0.5m]

Worsted-weight	YARN AMOUNT
□ White	36 yds. [32.9m]
■ Black	29 yds. [26.5m]
■ Pumpkin	5 yds. [4.6m]

STITCH KEY:
- ⊟ Backstitch/Straight
- ⊙ French Knot

Holder Assembly Illustration
(Pieces are shown in different colors for contrast; gray denotes wrong side.)

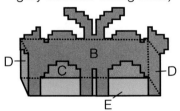

STAR COASTERS

SIZES
Each Coaster is 5⅛" x 5⅛" [13cm x 13cm]; Holder is 2¾" x 6" x 3" tall [7cm x 15.2cm x 7.6cm].

SKILL LEVEL: Average

MATERIALS
- One sheet of 5-mesh plastic canvas
- Metallic cord; for amount see Color Key.
- Worsted-weight or plastic canvas yarn; for amounts see Color Key on page 12.

CUTTING INSTRUCTIONS
A: For Coaster Fronts and Backings, cut eight (four for Fronts and four for Backings) according to graph.

B: For Holder Sides, cut two 27w x 14h-holes.

C: For Holder Ends, cut two 11w x 14h-holes.

D: For Holder Bottom, cut one 29w x 13h-holes.

STITCHING INSTRUCTIONS
NOTES: Backing A and D pieces are not worked. Use a doubled strand of yarn and cord throughout.

1: Using colors and stitches indicated, work

four A pieces for Fronts, B and C pieces according to graphs. Using white and French knot, embroider detail on Front A pieces as indicated on graph.

2: For each Coaster (make 4), holding one Backing A to wrong side of one Front A, with matching colors, whipstitch together.

3: For Holder, with white, whipstitch B and C pieces together as indicated and according to Holder Assembly Illustration; overcast unfinished edges.

—Designed by Jocelyn Sass

COLOR KEY: Star Coasters

	Metallic cord	AMOUNT
■	Red	45 yds. [41.1m]

	Worstedweight	YARN AMOUNT
▨	White	49 yds. [44.8m]
▨	Royal	25 yds. [22.9m]

OTHER:
- ⊙ French Knot
- ☐ End & Sides/Bottom Attachment

A – Coaster Front & Backing
(25w x 25h-hole pieces) Cut 8.
Work 4 for Fronts & leave 4
unworked for Backings.

C – Holder End
(11w x 14h-hole pieces)
Cut 2 & work.

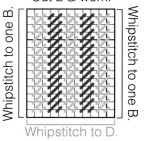

B – Holder Side
(27w x 14h-hole pieces) Cut 2 & work.

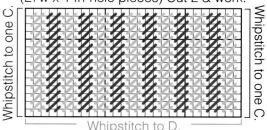

D – Holder Bottom
(29w x 13h-hole piece)
Cut 1 & leave unworked.

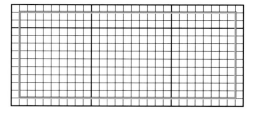

Holder Assembly Illustration
(Pieces are shown in different colors for
contrast; gray denotes wrong side.)

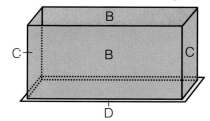

CANDLE COASTERS

SIZES
Each Coaster is 3¼" x 3¾" [8.2cm x 9.5cm]; Holder is 1½" x 3⅞" x 2" tall [3.8cm x 9.8cm x 5.1cm].

SKILL LEVEL: Average

MATERIALS
- One sheet of 7-mesh plastic canvas
- Worsted-weight or plastic canvas yarn; for amounts see Color Key.

CUTTING INSTRUCTIONS
A: For Coasters, cut four according to graph.
B: For Holder Front, cut one according to graph.
C: For Holder Back, cut one 24w x 9h-holes (no graph).
D: For Holder Sides, cut two 9w x 9h-holes (no graph).
E: For Holder Bottom, cut one 24w x 9h-holes (no graph).

STITCHING INSTRUCTIONS
NOTE: E is not worked.

1: Using colors and stitches indicated, work A and B pieces according to graphs; fill in uncoded areas and work C and D pieces using scarlet and continental stitch. With indicated and matching colors, overcast edges of A pieces.

2: Using colors (Separate into individual plies, if desired.) and embroidery stitches indicated, embroider detail on A pieces as indicated on graph.

3: With matching colors as shown in photo, whipstitch B-E pieces together as indicated and according to Holder Assembly Illustration; overcast unfinished edges.

—Designed by Terry A. Ricioli

COLOR KEY: Candle Coasters

Worsted-weight		YARN AMOUNT
☐	Scarlet	33 yds. [30.2m]
▨	Brisk Green	12 yds. [11m]
◼	Dk. Red	6 yds. [5.5m]
◼	Wine	5 yds. [4.6m]
▤	Daffodil	2 yds. [1.8m]
◼	Black	½ yd. [0.5m]

STITCH KEY:
⊟ Backstitch/Straight

A – Coaster
(21w x 24h-hole pieces) Cut 4 & work.

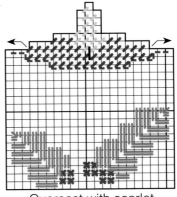

Overcast with scarlet between arrows.

B – Holder Front
(24w x 12h-hole piece) Cut 1 & work.

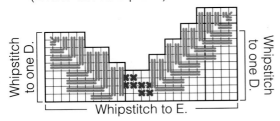

Whipstitch to one D.

Whipstitch to one D.

Whipstitch to E.

Holder Assembly Illustration
(Pieces are shown in different colors for contrast; gray denotes wrong side.)

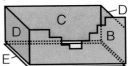

SOUTHWEST KITCHEN SET

Step into a world of warm sunsets and wide-open spaces with this kitchen set full of the glory of the Southwest.

SIZES

Each Canister Holder is 6⅝" square x 7" tall [16.8cm x 17.8cm] and holds a 39oz. coffee can; Plant Cozy is 6½" across x 6¾" tall [16.5cm x 17.1cm]; Place Mat is 10½" x 15⅞" [26.7cm x 40.3cm]; Napkin Ring is 2" x 2½" [5.1cm x 6.4cm]; each Coaster is 3¾" square [9.5cm]; Coaster Holder is 4¼" across x 1¾" tall [10.8cm x 4.4cm].

SKILL LEVEL: Average

MATERIALS
- Five sheets of 5-mesh plastic canvas
- Worsted-weight or plastic canvas yarn; for amounts see Color Key.

CUTTING INSTRUCTIONS
A: For Canister Holder Fronts #1-#3, cut

three (one for each Front) 32w x 34h-holes.

B: For Canister Holder Sides & Backs, cut nine (six for Sides and three for Backs) 32w x 34h-holes.

C: For Canister Holder Bottoms, cut three 32w x 32h-holes (no graph).

D: For Canister Holder Lids and Linings, cut six (three for Lids and three for Linings) 32w x 32h-holes.

E: For Canister Holder Lid Corner Bracket Pieces, cut twenty-four according to graph.

F: For Plant Cozy, cut one 101w x 33h-holes.

G: For Place Mat, cut one 78w x 52h-holes.

H: For Napkin Ring, cut one according to graph.

I: For Coaster Fronts and Backings, cut eight (four for Fronts and four for Backings) 18w x 18h-holes.

J: For Coaster Holder Sides, cut four 20w x 8h-holes (no graph).

K: For Coaster Holder Bottom, cut one 20w x 20h-holes (no graph).

STITCHING INSTRUCTIONS

NOTES: C, Lining D, E, Backing I, and K pieces are not worked.
Use a double strand of yarn throughout.

1: Using colors indicated and continental stitch, work A, B, three D pieces for Lids, F-H and four I pieces for Fronts according to graphs; using eggshell and continental stitch, work J pieces. With aqua for Plant Cozy, white for Napkin Ring and with matching colors for Place Mat, overcast edges.

2: For each Canister Holder (make 3), with aqua, whipstitch and assemble A-E pieces as indicated on graphs and according to Canister Holder Assembly Diagram on page 17.

COLOR KEY: Southwest Kitchen Set

Worsted-weight	YARN AMOUNT
Eggshell	8 oz. [226.8g]
Aqua	7 oz. [198.5g]
Dk. Orange	6½ oz. [184.3g]
Gold	6½ oz. [184.3g]

ATTACHMENT:

☐ Corner Bracket

3: For each Coaster (make 4), holding one Backing I to wrong side of one Front I, with eggshell, whipstitch together.

4: For Coaster Holder, with eggshell, whipstitch J and K pieces together according to Coaster Holder Assembly Illustration on page 17; overcast unfinished edges.

—Designed by Eleanor Albano

A – Canister Holder Front #1
(32w x 34h-hole piece) Cut 1 & work.

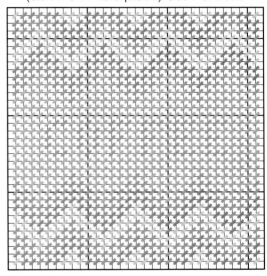

A – Canister Holder Front #2
(32w x 34h-hole piece) Cut 1 & work.

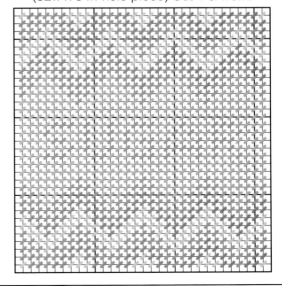

A – Canister Holder Front #3
(32w x 34h-hole piece) Cut 1 & work.

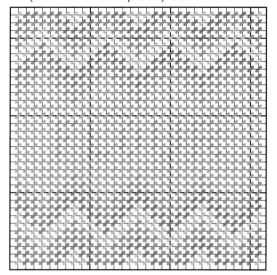

I – Coaster Front & Backing
(18w x 18h-hole pieces) Cut 8.
Work 4 for Fronts & leave 4
unworked for Backings.

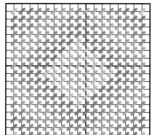

COLOR KEY: Southwest Kitchen Set

Worsted-weight	YARN AMOUNT
Eggshell	8 oz. [226.8g]
Aqua	7 oz. [198.5g]
Dk. Orange	6½ oz. [184.3g]
Gold	6½ oz. [184.3g]

ATTACHMENT:
☐ Corner Bracket

D – Canister Holder Lid & Lining
(32w x 32h-hole pieces) Cut 6.
Work 3 for Lids & leave 3 unworked for Linings.

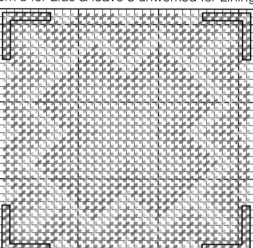

E – Canister Holder Lid Corner Bracket Piece
(6w x 7h-hole pieces)
Cut 24 & leave unworked.

Whipstitch to Lining D.

Whipstitch to one E.

F – Plant Cozy
(101w x 33h-hole piece) Cut 1 & work,
overlapping ends & working through both
thicknesses at overlap area to join.

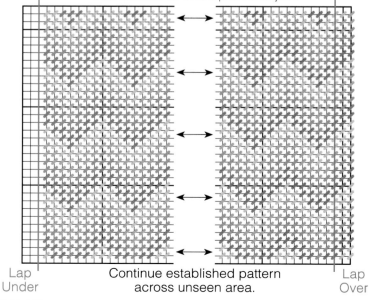

Lap Under

Continue established pattern
across unseen area.

Lap Over

B – Canister Holder Sides & Backs
(32w x 34h-hole piece) Cut 9. Work 6 for
Sides & 3 for Backs.

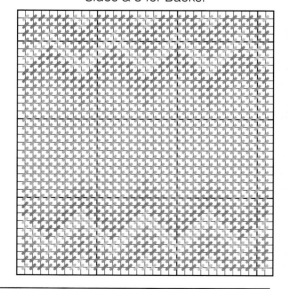

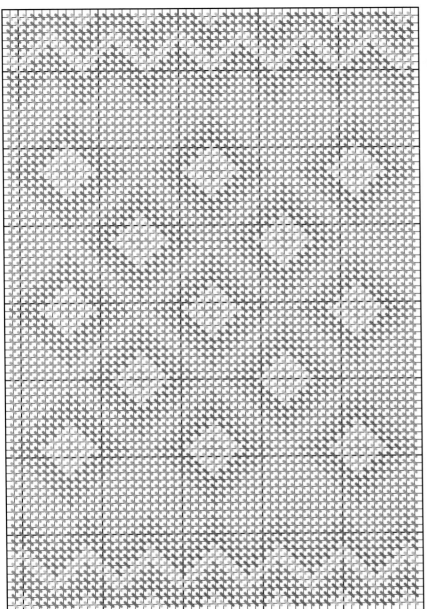

G – Place Mat
(78w x 52h-hole piece) Cut 1 & work.

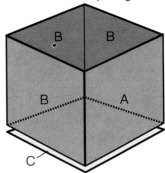

Canister Holder Assembly Diagram
(Pieces are shown in different colors for contrast.)

Step 1:
Whipstitch A-C pieces together, overcast unfinished top edges.

Step 2:
Whipstitch E pieces together & to Lining D; do not overcast unfinished edges of Corner Bracket Pieces.

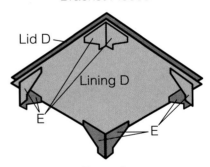

Step 3:
Holding Lining D to wrong side of Lid D, whipstitch together.

H – Napkin Ring
(34w x 11h-hole piece) Cut 1 & work, overlapping ends & working through both thicknesses at overlap area to join.

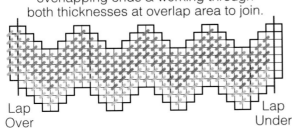

Lap Over

Lap Under

Coaster Holder Assembly Illustration
(Pieces are shown in different colors for contrast; gray denotes wrong side.)

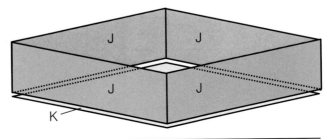

CHICKEN BLACKBOARD

*You'll never have to leave hen-scratched notes
lying around with this useful and reusable blackboard.*

SIZE
10⅝" x 14" [27cm x 35.6cm] with a 3¾" x 5⅜"
[9.5cm x 13.7cm] window.

SKILL LEVEL: Easy

MATERIALS
• One 12" x 18" [30.5cm x 45.7cm] or larger
  sheet of 7-mesh plastic canvas

• One 5" x 7" [12.7cm x 17.8cm] blackboard
• One 11mm x 15mm blue paste-on wiggle eye
• Craft glue or glue gun
• Worsted-weight or plastic canvas yarn; for
  amounts see Color Key.

CUTTING INSTRUCTIONS
For Chicken, cut one according to graph.

STITCHING INSTRUCTIONS

1: Using colors and stitches indicated, work Chicken according to graph. With sail blue for cutout and body and with matching colors, overcast edges.

2: Glue eye to Chicken as shown in photo; glue blackboard to back over cutout. Hang or display as desired.

—Designed by Michele Wilcox

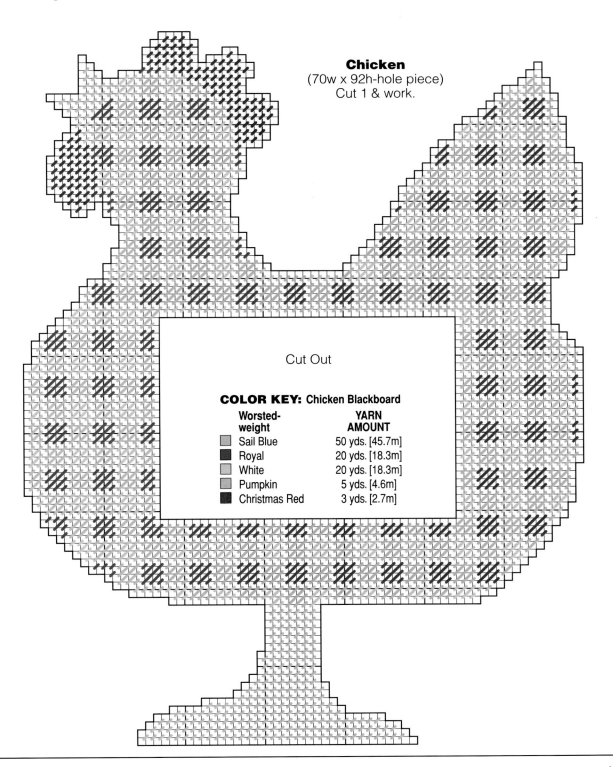

Chicken
(70w x 92h-hole piece)
Cut 1 & work.

Cut Out

COLOR KEY: Chicken Blackboard

Worsted-weight	YARN AMOUNT
Sail Blue	50 yds. [45.7m]
Royal	20 yds. [18.3m]
White	20 yds. [18.3m]
Pumpkin	5 yds. [4.6m]
Christmas Red	3 yds. [2.7m]

PATCHWORK KITCHEN TRIO

Fill your kitchen with the warmth and country-goodness of these patchwork accessories.

SIZES

Trivet is 8½" square [21.6cm]; Box is 8" square x 5½" tall [20.3cm x 14cm]; Napkin Holder is 3" x 5½" x 5½" tall [7.6cm x 14cm x 14cm].

SKILL LEVEL: Average

MATERIALS

- 5½ sheets of clear 7-mesh plastic canvas
- Worsted-weight or plastic canvas yarn; for amounts see Color Key.

CUTTING INSTRUCTIONS

A: For Trivet Front and Backing, cut two (one for Front and one for Backing) 55w x 55h-holes.

B: For Box Wide Sides and Linings, cut eight (four for Sides and four for Linings) 35w x 35h-holes.

C: For Box Narrow Sides and Linings, cut eight (four for Sides and four for Linings) 12w x 35h-holes.

D: For Box Bottom, cut one according to graph.

A – Trivet Front & Backing
(55w x 55h-hole pieces) Cut 2.
Work 1 for Front & leave 1 unworked for Backing.

COLOR KEY: Patchwork Kitchen Trio

Worsted-weight	YARN AMOUNT
Lemon	60 yds. [54.9m]
Sandstone	32 yds. [29.3m]
Yellow	32 yds. [29.3m]
Rust	20 yds. [18.3m]
Tangerine	18 yds. [16.5m]

C – Box Narrow Side & Linir
(12w x 35h-hole pieces) Cut 8.
Work 4 for Sides & leave 4 unwork
for Linings.

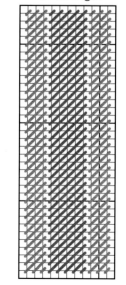

E: For Napkin Holder Outer Sides and Linings, cut four (two for Sides and two for Linings) 35w x 35h-holes (no graph).

F: For Napkin Holder Inner sides, cut two 20w x 23h-holes (no graph).

G: For Napkin Holder Inner Ends, cut two according to graph.

H: For Napkin Holder Inner Bottom Pieces, cut one 12w x 23h-holes for Narrow Bottom and one 18w x 24h-holes for Wide Bottom (no graphs).

STITCHING INSTRUCTIONS

NOTE: Backing A, Lining B, Lining C, D, Lining E and F-H pieces are not worked.

1: For Trivet, using colors and stitches indicated, work Front A according to graph. Holding Backing A to wrong side of Front, with lemon, whipstitch together.

2: For Box, using colors and stitches indicated, work four B and four C pieces according to graphs. Holding Lining pieces to wrong side of matching worked pieces, with lemon, whipstitch B-D pieces together through all thicknesses as needed to join according to Box Assembly Illustration on page 22. Whipstitch unfinished top edges together.

3: For Napkin Holder, using colors and stitches indicated, work four E pieces according to B graph. With lemon, whipstitch E-H pieces together according to Napkin Holder Assembly Diagram on page 22.

—Designed by Carol Nartowicz

B – Box Wide Side & Lining
(35w x 35h-hole pieces) Cut 8.
Work 4 for Sides & leave 4 unworked for Linings.

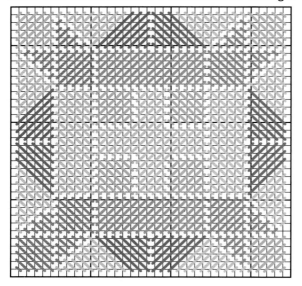

Napkin Holder Assembly Diagram
(Pieces are shown in different colors for contrast; gray denotes wrong side.)

Step 1:
Whipstitch F-H pieces together, forming Inner Holder.

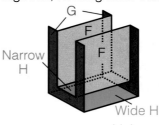

Step 2:
Whipstitch G & Lining E pieces together.

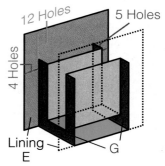

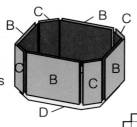

Step 3:
Holding E pieces wrong sides together, whipstitch together, catching center bottom edge of Inner Holder to join as you work; do not overcast unfinished edges.

Box Assembly Illustration
(Lining pieces are shown in red for contrast; gray denotes wrong side.)

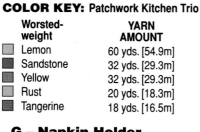

D – Box Bottom
(53w x 53h-hole piece) Cut 1 & leave unworked.

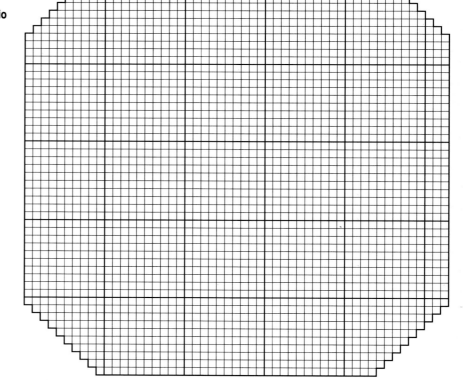

COLOR KEY: Patchwork Kitchen Trio

Worsted-weight		YARN AMOUNT
	Lemon	60 yds. [54.9m]
	Sandstone	32 yds. [29.3m]
	Yellow	32 yds. [29.3m]
	Rust	20 yds. [18.3m]
	Tangerine	18 yds. [16.5m]

G – Napkin Holder Inner End
(18w x 23h-hole pieces) Cut 2 & leave unworked.

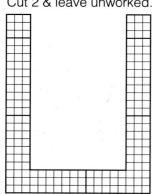

FANCIFUL FRUIT BOXES

*Four fresh and tasteful fruit boxes look simply delicious and are
great for tucking away pre-ripened fruit, pasta, cookies and other kitchen goodies.*

SIZE
Each is 6¾" across x 2¼" tall [17.1cm x 5.7cm].

SKILL LEVEL: Average

MATERIALS FOR ONE
- Two 6" [15.2cm] plastic canvas heart shapes
- One sheet of 7-mesh plastic canvas
- Scraps of 10-mesh plastic canvas (for Lemon, Apple or Watermelon Box)
- Craft glue or glue gun
- Heavy metallic braid or metallic cord; for amounts see individual Color Keys.
- Worsted-weight or plastic canvas yarn; for amounts see individual Color Keys.

LEMON
CUTTING INSTRUCTIONS
A: For Lemon Lid Top, use one heart shape.

B: For Lemon Lid Sides, cut two from 7-mesh 64w x 5h-holes (no graph).

C: For Lemon Box Sides, cut two from 7-mesh 60w x 13h-holes (no graph).

D: For Lemon Box Bottom, cut away one outer row of holes from remaining heart shape (no graph).

E: For Lemon Flowers, cut two from 7-mesh according to graph.

F: For Lemon Leaf, cut one from 7-mesh according to graph.

G: For Lemon Seeds, cut ten from 10-mesh according to graph.

STITCHING INSTRUCTIONS
NOTE: D piece is not worked.

1: Using colors and stitches indicated, work A, F and G pieces according to graphs; work B and C pieces according to Lemon Lid & Box Side Stitch Pattern Guide. With white for Lemon Flowers and with matching colors, overcast edges of E-G pieces.

2: Using braid or cord and embroidery stitches indicated, embroider detail on A and E pieces as indicated on graphs.

3: With yellow, whipstitch A and B pieces together according to Lid Assembly Illustration on page 26, and C and D pieces together according to Box Assembly Illustration; overcast unfinished edges of Box and Lid.

4: Glue Flowers, Leaf and Seeds to Lid as shown in photo.

STRAWBERRY
CUTTING INSTRUCTIONS
A-D: Follow Steps A-D of Lemon.

E: For Strawberry Flower, cut one from 7-mesh according to graph.

F: For Strawberry Stem, cut one from 7-mesh according to graph.

STITCHING INSTRUCTIONS
NOTE: D piece is not worked.

1: Using colors and stitches indicated, work A, E and F pieces according to graphs; work B and C pieces according to Strawberry Lid & Box Side Stitch Pattern Guide. With matching colors, overcast edges of E and F pieces.

2: Using braid or cord and embroidery stitches indicated, embroider detail on A and E pieces as indicated on graphs.

3: Substituting red for yellow, follow Step 3 of Lemon. Glue Flower and Stem to Lid as shown in photo.

APPLE
CUTTING INSTRUCTIONS
A-D: Follow Steps A-D of Lemon.

E: For Apple Flower, cut one from 7-mesh according to graph.

F: For Apple Leaf, cut one from 7-mesh according to Lemon F graph.

G: For Apple Seeds, cut five from 10-mesh according to graph.

STITCHING INSTRUCTIONS
NOTE: D piece is not worked.

1: Using colors and stitches indicated, work A, E, F (substitute holly for forest) and G pieces according to graphs; work B and C pieces according to Apple Lid and Box Side Stitch Pattern Guide. With matching colors, overcast edges of E-G pieces.

2: Using braid or cord and embroidery stitches indicated, embroider detail on E as indicated on graph.

3: Substituting red for yellow, follow Step 3 of Lemon. Glue Flower, Leaf and Seeds to Lid as shown in photo.

WATERMELON
CUTTING INSTRUCTIONS
A: Follow Step A of Lemon.

B: For Watermelon Lid Sides, cut two from 7-mesh 64w x 6h-holes (no graph).

C-D: Follow Steps C-D of Lemon.

E: For Watermelon Seeds, cut twelve from 10-mesh according to graph.

STITCHING INSTRUCTIONS
NOTE: D piece is not worked.

1: Using colors and stitches indicated, work A and E pieces according to graphs; work B and C pieces according to Watermelon Lid & Box Side Stitch Pattern Guide. With braid or cord, overcast edges of E pieces.

2: Substituting fern for yellow, follow Step 3 of Lemon. Glue Seeds to lid as shown in photo.

—Designed by Vicki Blizzard

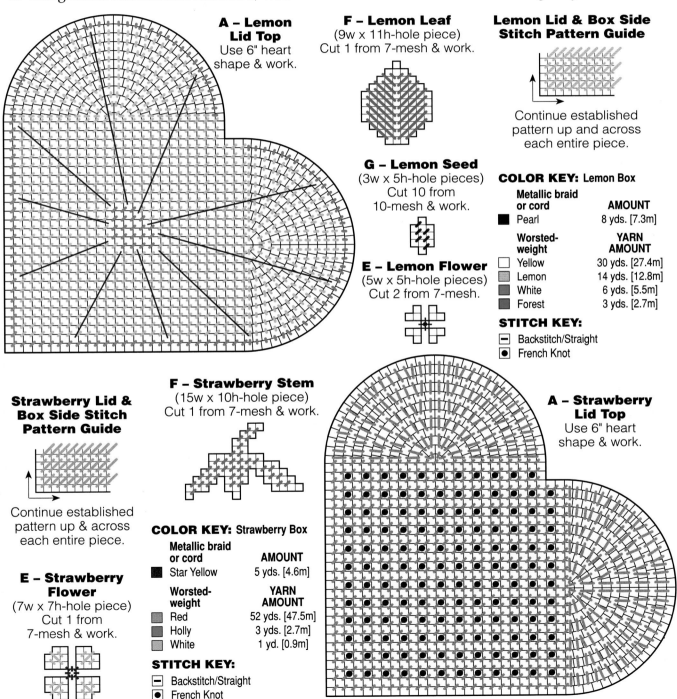

A – Lemon Lid Top
Use 6" heart shape & work.

F – Lemon Leaf
(9w x 11h-hole piece)
Cut 1 from 7-mesh & work.

G – Lemon Seed
(3w x 5h-hole pieces)
Cut 10 from 10-mesh & work.

E – Lemon Flower
(5w x 5h-hole pieces)
Cut 2 from 7-mesh.

Lemon Lid & Box Side Stitch Pattern Guide

Continue established pattern up and across each entire piece.

COLOR KEY: Lemon Box

Metallic braid or cord	AMOUNT
■ Pearl	8 yds. [7.3m]

Worsted-weight	YARN AMOUNT
□ Yellow	30 yds. [27.4m]
Lemon	14 yds. [12.8m]
White	6 yds. [5.5m]
Forest	3 yds. [2.7m]

STITCH KEY:
- ⊟ Backstitch/Straight
- ⊙ French Knot

Strawberry Lid & Box Side Stitch Pattern Guide

Continue established pattern up & across each entire piece.

E – Strawberry Flower
(7w x 7h-hole piece)
Cut 1 from 7-mesh & work.

F – Strawberry Stem
(15w x 10h-hole piece)
Cut 1 from 7-mesh & work.

COLOR KEY: Strawberry Box

Metallic braid or cord	AMOUNT
■ Star Yellow	5 yds. [4.6m]

Worsted-weight	YARN AMOUNT
Red	52 yds. [47.5m]
Holly	3 yds. [2.7m]
White	1 yd. [0.9m]

STITCH KEY:
- ⊟ Backstitch/Straight
- ⊙ French Knot

A – Strawberry Lid Top
Use 6" heart shape & work.

COLOR KEY: Apple Box

Metallic braid or cord	AMOUNT
Bronze	2 yds. [1.8m]
Star Yellow	1 yd. [0.9m]

Worsted-weight	YARN AMOUNT
Red	33 yds. [30.2m]
White	12 yds. [11m]
Holly	2 yds. [1.8m]
Flesh Tone	1 yd. [0.9m]

STITCH KEY:

- ⊟ Backstitch/Straight
- ● French Knot

G – Apple Seed
(3w x 4h- hole pieces)
Cut 5 from
10-mesh & work.

Apple Lid & Box Side Stitch Pattern Guide

Continue established pattern up & across each entire piece.

E – Apple Flower
(7w x 7h-hole piece)
Cut 1 from
7-mesh & work.

E – Watermelon Seed
(5w x 6h-hole pieces)
Cut 12 from
10-mesh & work.

COLOR KEY: Watermelon Box

Metallic braid or cord	AMOUNT
Black	8 yds. [7.3m]

Worsted-weight	YARN AMOUNT
Holly	25 yds. [22.9m]
Fern	17 yds. [15.5m]
Watermelon	10 yds. [9.1m]
Flesh Tone	5 yds. [4.6m]
White	3 yds. [2.7m]

Watermelon Lid & Box Side Stitch Pattern Guide

Continue established pattern up & across each entire piece.

Lid Assembly Illustration
(Underside view; gray denotes wrong side.)

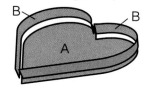

Box Assembly Illustration
(Gray denotes wrong side.)

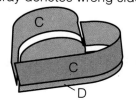

POTPOURRI PIES

Make some aroma-filled pies to please the entire household.
The best part is you won't have to spend hours in the kitchen to bake them!

SIZES
Pie is 9" across x about 4" tall [22.9cm x 10.2cm]; Tart is 5" across x about 3" tall [12.7cm x 7.6cm].

SKILL LEVEL: Average

MATERIALS
- One sheet of 7-mesh plastic canvas
- Two 9½" [24.1cm] plastic canvas radial circles
- One each 9" [22.9cm] and 5" [12.7cm] aluminum pie pans
- One 14mm and two 18mm amethyst large hole ball beads
- 7" [17.8cm] of 20-gauge wire
- Three 3" [7.6cm] lengths of green plastic-covered stem wire (from artificial flowers)
- Floral tape
- Bunch of dried berries
- Assorted dried leaves, flowers and seed pods

- Five cups of potpourri
- Craft glue or glue gun
- Raffia straw; for amounts see Color Key.

CUTTING INSTRUCTIONS

A: For Pie Edge and Lining, cut two (one for Edge and one for Lining) from 9½" circles according to graph.

B: For Pie Large Strips, cut two according to graph.

C: For Pie Medium Strips, cut four according to graph.

D: For Pie Small Strips, cut four according to graph.

E: For Leaf #1, cut one according to graph.

F: For Leaf #2, cut one according to graph.

G: For Tart Edge and Lining, cut two (one for Edge and one for Lining) from 9½" circles according to graph.

H: For Tart Large Strips, cut two according to graph.

I: For Tart Small Strips, cut four according to graph.

J: For Apple Slice, cut one according to graph.

STITCHING INSTRUCTIONS

NOTE: Lining A and Lining G pieces are not worked.

1: Using colors and stitches indicated, work one A for Pie Edge, B-F, one G for Tart Edge and H-J pieces according to graphs; overcast long edges of B-D, H and I pieces. With indicated and matching colors overcast edges of J.

NOTE: Cut 20-gauge wire into two 3½ [8.9cm] lengths.

2: Using Christmas green and stitches indicated, holding one wire to back of one leaf center, work E and F pieces over wire according to graphs.

3: Weaving B-D pieces together as shown in photo and holding ends between A pieces as indicated, with tan, whipstitch A-D pieces together through all thicknesses around outer edges. Fill 9" [22.9cm] pie pan with potpourri and glue Pie Edge Lining to pie pan edge.

4: Weaving H and I pieces together as shown and holding ends between G pieces as indicated, with tan, whipstitch G-I pieces together through all thicknesses around outer edges. Fill 5" [12.7cm] pie pan with potpourri and glue Tart Edge Lining to pie pan edge.

5: For each Cherry (make 3), glue one end of one 3" [7.6cm] stem wire inside one bead. With floral tape, wrap stems together.

6: Twist wire stem of E around wire stem of F. Shape leaves as desired. Glue Leaves, Cherries and dried berries to Pie top and Apple Slice and dried embellishments to Tart top as shown.

—*Designed by Diane T. Ray*

J – Apple Slice
(17w x 5h-hole piece)
Cut 1 & work.

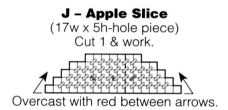

Overcast with red between arrows.

A – Pie Edge & Lining
Cut 1 from each circle.
Work 1 for Pie Edge & leave 1 unworked for Pie Edge Lining.

G – Tart Edge & Lining
Cut 1 each from 9½" circle.
Work 1 for Tart Edge & 1 for Tart Edge Lining.

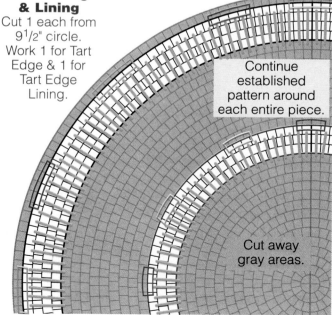

Continue established pattern around each entire piece.

Cut away gray areas.

B – Pie Large Strip
(65w x 6h-hole pieces) Cut 2 & work.

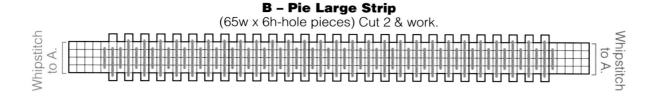

Whipstitch to A.

Whipstitch to A.

C – Pie Medium Strip
(61w x 6h-hole pieces) Cut 4 & work.

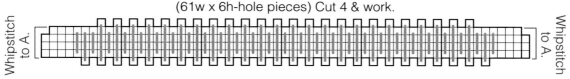

Whipstitch to A.

Whipstitch to A.

D – Pie Small Strip
(47w x 6h-hole pieces) Cut 4 & work.

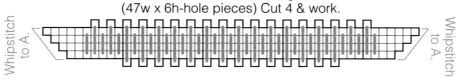

Whipstitch to A.

Whipstitch to A.

COLOR KEY: Potpourri Pies

Raffia straw		AMOUNT
 Tan		65 yds. [59.4m]
Christmas Green		5 yds. [4.6m]
Eggshell		1 1/2 yds. [1.4m]
Brown		1/2 yd. [0.5m]
Red		1/2 yd. [0.5m]

OTHER:
- ⊟ Backstitch/Straight
- ☐ Pie Large Strip Attachment
- ☐ Pie Medium Strip Attachment
- ☐ Pie Small Strip Attachment
- ☐ Tart Large Strip Attachment
- ☐ Tart Small Strip Attachment

H – Tart Large Strip
(39w x 4h-hole pieces) Cut 2 & work.

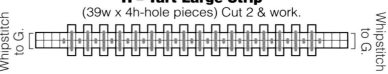

Whipstitch to G.

Whipstitch to G.

I – Tart Small Strip
(35w x 4h-hole pieces) Cut 4 & work.

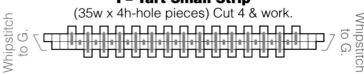

Whipstitch to G.

Whipstitch to G.

E – Leaf #1
(18w x 18h-hole piece) Cut 1.
Hold one 3 1/2" wire to canvas
& work over wire.

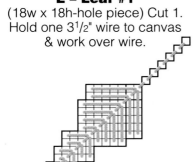

F – Leaf #2
(13w x 13h-hole piece) Cut 1.
Hold one 3 1/2" wire to canvas &
work over wire.

KITCHEN HELPERS

*Need an extra pair of hands? These delightful
mitts and helpful pals are perfect for placing utensils in a handy spot.*

SIZE

Each Mitt is 8¼" x 10⅝" [21cm x 27cm], not
including hanger and embellishments.

SKILL LEVEL: Average

MATERIALS

- Six sheets of 7-mesh plastic canvas
- ¼ yd. [0.2m] each red and green ⅛" [3mm]
  satin ribbon
- Artificial pine greenery

- Blue eucalyptus stems
- Three cinnamon sticks
- Two small wire whisks
- One wooden spoon
- Two 1" [2.5cm] plastic rings
- Polyester fiberfill
- Craft glue or glue gun
- Worsted-weight or plastic canvas yarn; for amounts see Color Key.

CUTTING INSTRUCTIONS

A: For Red and Blue Mitt Fronts and Backs, cut four (two for Fronts and two for Backs) according to graph.

B: For Red and Blue Cuff Fronts and Backings, cut four (two for Fronts and two for Backings) 45w x 15h-holes.

C: For Red and Blue Hangers, cut two (one for Red Hanger and one for Blue Hanger) according to graph.

D: For Gingerbread Cookies, cut two according to graph.

E: For Duck, cut one according to graph.

F: For Pig, cut one according to graph.

STITCHING INSTRUCTIONS

NOTE: Back A and Backing B pieces are not worked.

1: Using colors and stitches indicated, work two of each A and B pieces for Fronts and C pieces according to graphs.

2: Using rust for Gingerbread Cookies, beige for Duck and Pig and continental stitch,

work D-F pieces; with matching colors, overcast edges.

3: Using colors and embroidery stitches indicated, embroider detail on B and D-F pieces as indicated on graphs. Tie each ribbon into a bow; glue one to each Gingerbread Cookie as shown in photo.

4: For each Mitt (make 2), holding one Back A to wrong side of one Front A, with matching colors as shown, whipstitch together as indicated; do not overcast unfinished edge.

5: For each Cuff (make 2), holding one Backing B to wrong side of one Front B, with matching colors, whipstitch short ends together, catching ends of corresponding Hanger as indicated as you work (see photo); overcast unfinished edges of Front B and Hanger. For each Mitt, slip corresponding Cuff over top of Mitt as shown and glue to secure.

6: Arrange greenery, eucalyptus stems, cinnamon sticks, whisks and spoon inside each Mitt as shown or as desired. Glue Gingerbread Cookies, Duck and Pig to greenery and eucalyptus stems. Glue one plastic ring to back and hang as desired.

—*Designed by Robin Will*

COLOR KEY: Kitchen Helpers

Worsted-weight		YARN AMOUNT
▨	White	54 yds. [49.4m]
■	Christmas Red	27 yds. [24.7m]
☐	Sail Blue	27 yds. [24.7m]
☐	Rust	22 yds. [20.1m]
☐	Beige	15 yds. [13.7m]
▨	Christmas Green	12 yds. [11m]
☐	Lavender	12 yds. [11m]
■	Brown	3 yds. [2.7m]

STITCH KEY:

- ⊟ Backstitch/Straight
- ⦿ French Knot

D – Gingerbread Cookie
(28w x 37h-hole pieces) Cut 2.

E – Duck
(24w x 32h-hole piece) Cut 1.

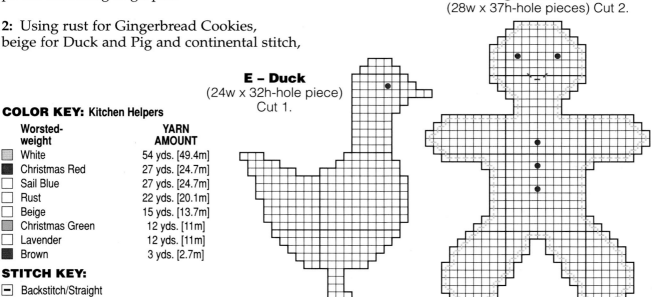

COLOR KEY: Kitchen Helpers

Worsted-weight	YARN AMOUNT
White	54 yds. [49.4m]
Christmas Red	27 yds. [24.7m]
Sail Blue	27 yds. [24.7m]
Rust	22 yds. [20.1m]
Beige	15 yds. [13.7m]
Christmas Green	12 yds. [11m]
Lavender	12 yds. [11m]
Brown	3 yds. [2.7m]

STITCH KEY:
- ▬ Backstitch/Straight
- ⊙ French Knot

B – Red & Blue Cuff Front & Backing
(45w x 15h-hole pieces) Cut 4.
Work 1 for Red Cuff Front; substituting lavender for
Christmas green & sail blue for Christmas red, work 1
for Blue Cuff Front. Leave 2 unworked for Backings.

Whipstitch to one C.

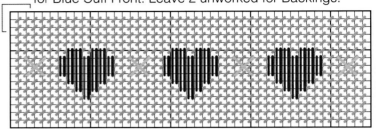

A – Red & Blue Mitt Front & Back
(55w x 66h-hole pieces) Cut 4.
Work 1 for Red Mitt Front; substituting sail blue for Christmas red,
work 1 for Blue Mitt Front. Leave 2 unworked for Backs.

Whipstitch between arrows.

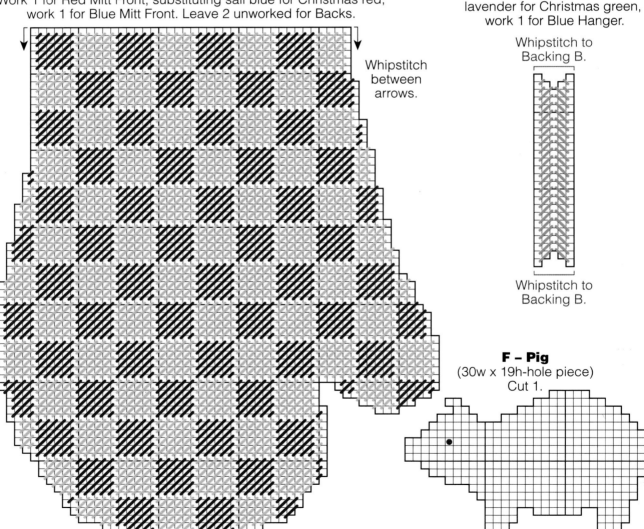

C – Red & Blue Hanger
(5w x 25h-hole pieces) Cut 2.
Work 1 for Red Hanger; substituting
lavender for Christmas green,
work 1 for Blue Hanger.

Whipstitch to Backing B.

Whipstitch to Backing B.

F – Pig
(30w x 19h-hole piece) Cut 1.

Chapter Two
GARDENS IN A HURRY

SUMMER HELPERS

When the weather starts to sizzle, stitch up these
quick-and-breezy accents to lift your patio or garden out of the doldrums.

QUICK-FOLD BASKETS

SIZE
3" x 4¼" [7.6cm x 10.8cm].

SKILL LEVEL: Easy

MATERIALS FOR ONE
- ½ sheet of clear or colored 7-mesh plastic canvas
- 1 yd. [0.9m] matching-color ¼" [6mm] satin ribbon
- Worsted-weight or plastic canvas yarn; for amount see Color Key.

CUTTING INSTRUCTIONS
For Basket, cut one according to graph.

STITCHING INSTRUCTIONS
NOTE: Colored canvas baskets may be left unworked.

1: Using color of choice and stitches indicated and leaving uncoded center area unworked, work Basket according to graph; overcast unfinished edges.

NOTE: Cut ribbon in half.

2: Assemble Basket and ribbons according to Quick-Fold Basket Assembly Diagram.

—*Designed by Carol Nartowicz*

Quick-Fold Basket Assembly Diagram
(Gray denotes wrong side.)

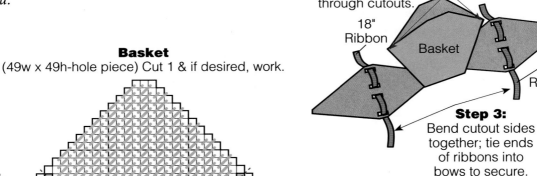

Step 1: Bring solid sides together; tack at corners to secure.

Step 2: Weave ribbons through cutouts.

18" Ribbon

Basket

18" Ribbon

Step 3: Bend cutout sides together; tie ends of ribbons into bows to secure.

Basket
(49w x 49h-hole piece) Cut 1 & if desired, work.

Cut out gray areas.

Cut through bars carefully.

COLOR KEY: Quick-Fold Baskets

Worsted-weight	YARN AMOUNT
■ Color of choice	20 yds. [18.3m]

SPARKLING PASTELS

SIZES
Tray is 1½" x 6" x 15⅜" [3.8cm x 15.2cm x 39.1cm]; Each Planter is 4⅜" across x 4¼" tall [11.1cm x 10.8cm].

SKILL LEVEL: Average

MATERIALS
- One 12" x 18" [30.5cm x 45.7cm] or larger sheet of 7-mesh plastic canvas
- Three sheets of light blue 7-mesh plastic canvas
- Three 4¼" [10.8cm] crafty circles
- Craft glue or glue gun
- ⅛" [3mm] metallic ribbon or metallic cord; for amounts see Color Key.
- Worsted-weight or plastic canvas yarn; for amounts see Color Key.

CUTTING INSTRUCTIONS
NOTE: Use light blue canvas for E pieces and lining A-C pieces.

A: For Tray Sides and Linings, cut four (two for Sides and two for Linings) 80w x 8h-holes (no graphs).

B: For Tray Ends and Linings, cut four (two for Ends and two for Linings) 18w x 8h-holes (no graphs).

C: For Tray End Corners and Linings, cut eight (four for Corners and four for Linings) 14w x 8h-holes (no graphs).

D: For Tray Bottom and Lining, cut two (one for Bottom and one for Lining) according to graph.

E: For Planter Sides, cut six 47w x 27h holes (no graph).

F: For Planter Bands, cut three 100w x 8h holes (no graph).

G: For Planter Bottoms, use crafty circles (no graph).

STITCHING INSTRUCTIONS
NOTES: D, E, G and Linings A-C are not worked. Use continental stitch throughout.

1: Using colors indicated, work A and F (Overlap two holes at ends of each F and work though both thicknesses at overlap areas to join.) pieces according to Tray & Planter Stitch Pattern Guide. Using white, work B and C pieces. With sail blue, overcast unfinished edges of F pieces.

2: Using blue metallic ribbon and French knot, embroider flower centers on A and F pieces as indicated on Tray & Planter Stitch Pattern Guide.

3: For Tray, holding one Lining to wrong side of each corresponding worked piece, with white, whipstitch side edges of A pieces together through all thicknesses according to Tray Assembly Illustration. With sail blue, whipstitch side assembly and D pieces together through all thicknesses (See Tray Assembly Illustration.); whipstitch unfinished top edges together.

4: For each Planter (make 3), with sail blue, whipstitch and assemble two E, one F and one G pieces according to Planter Assembly Diagram.

—*Designed by Trudy Bath Smith*

COLOR KEY: Sparkling Pastels

⅛" metallic ribbon or cord	AMOUNT
Green	10 yds. [9.1m]
Pink	9 yds. [8.2m]
Blue	5 yds. [4.6m]

Worsted-weight	YARN AMOUNT
White	2 oz. [56.7g]
Sail Blue	33 yds. [30.2m]

STITCH KEY:
- ● French Knot

Tray Assembly Illustration

(Pieces are shown in different colors for contrast; gray denotes wrong side.)

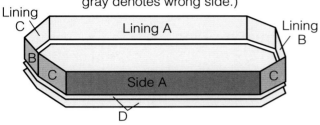

Lining C

Lining A

Lining B

B

C

Side A

C

D

Tray & Planter Stitch Pattern Guide

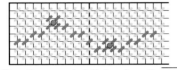

Continue established pattern across each entire piece.

Planter Assembly Diagram

(Pieces are shown in different colors for contrast; gray denotes wrong side.)

Step 1:
Overlapping two holes at each end of E pieces, whipstitch planter sides together.

F

E

E

G

Step 2:
Whipstitch side & G together.

Step 3:
Matching top edges, glue F to side.

D – Tray Bottom & Lining
(38w x 100h-hole pieces)
Cut 1 each & leave unworked.

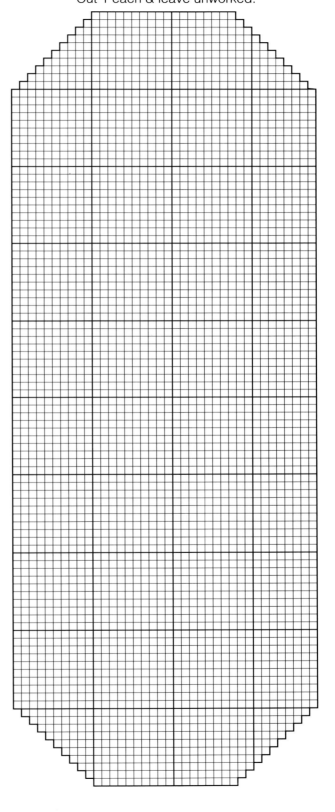

FLORAL FANTASY

Romance your decor with these fabulous floral accents for your bath.

SIZES
Box is 4⅝" square x 4" tall [11.7cm x 10.2cm]; Tissue Holder holds a standard-size roll of bathroom tissue.

SKILL LEVEL: Easy

MATERIALS
- One 12" x 18" [30.5cm x 45.7cm] or larger sheet of pink 7-mesh plastic canvas
- ½ sheet of standard-size pink 7-mesh plastic canvas
- Craft glue or glue gun
- Worsted-weight or plastic canvas yarn; for amounts see Color Key.

CUTTING INSTRUCTIONS
   A: For Box Sides, cut four according to graph.
   B: For Box Bottom, cut one 30w x 30h-holes (no graph).
   C: For Tissue Holder Side, cut one according to graph.
   D: For Tissue Holder Handle Pieces, cut two according to graph.

STITCHING INSTRUCTIONS
NOTE: B is not worked.

1: Using colors and stitches indicated and leaving uncoded areas of A and C unworked, work A, C and D pieces according to graphs.

2: With Christmas green for Tissue Holder short ends and with matching colors as shown in photo, overcast indicated and cutout edges of A and C and edges of D pieces.

3: For Box, with sail blue, whipstitch A and B pieces together according to Box Assembly Illustration; overcast unfinished top edges.

4: For Tissue Holder, glue one D piece to wrong side of each end of C as indicated and as shown in photo. Hang as desired.

—*Designed by Michele Wilcox*

C – Tissue Holder Side

(30w x 120h-hole piece) Cut 1 & work.
Overcast between arrows.

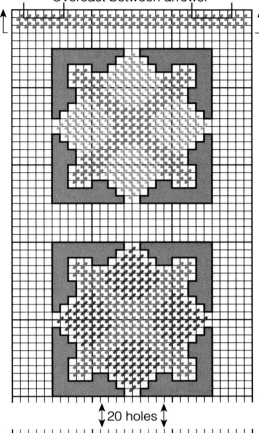

↕20 holes↕

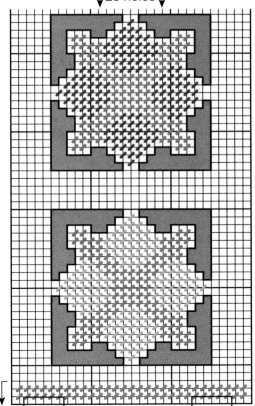

A – Box Side

(30w x 26h-hole pieces)
Cut 4. Work 2; substituting sail
blue for lilac, work 2.

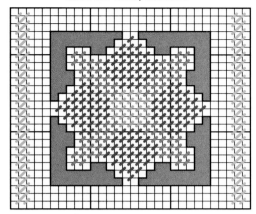

Cut out gray areas.

COLOR KEY: Floral Fantasy

Worsted-weight	YARN AMOUNT
☐ Sail Blue	30 yds. [27.4m]
☐ Christmas Green	25 yds. [22.9m]
☐ Lilac	14 yds. [12.8m]
☐ Eggshell	4 yds. [3.7m]

PLACEMENT KEY:

⊟ Handle

D – Tissue Holder Handle Piece

(25w x 17h-hole pieces)
Cut 2 & work.

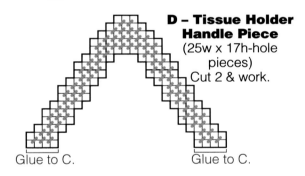

Glue to C.   Glue to C.

Box Assembly Illustration

(Gray denotes wrong side.)

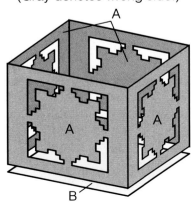

A

A

A

B

IN MY GARDEN

Sunny sunflowers grace these hang-ups,
fit for anyone who appreciates nature's beauty.

SIZES
Wall Hanging is 4½" x 11" tall [11.4cm x 27.9cm], not including raffia; Door Hanger is 5½" x 8¾" [14cm x 22.2cm], not including bow.

SKILL LEVEL: Average

MATERIALS
- 1½ sheets of 7-mesh plastic canvas
- 2 yds. [1.8m] of natural raffia
- Craft glue or glue gun
- No. 3 pearl cotton or six-strand embroidery floss; for amount see Color Key.
- Worsted-weight or plastic canvas yarn; for amounts see Color Key.

CUTTING INSTRUCTIONS
  A: For Wall Hanging Back, cut one according to graph.
  B: For Sunflower, cut one according to graph.
  C: For Leaves, cut four according to graph.
  D: For Stem, cut one 1w x 29h-holes (no graph).
  E: For Pot, cut one according to graph.
  F: For Door Hanger, cut one according to graph.

STITCHING INSTRUCTIONS
1: Using colors and stitches indicated, work A-C, E and F pieces according to graphs; fill in uncoded areas of F using eggshell and continental stitch. With holly for Stem and with matching colors, overcast edges of pieces.

2: Using pearl cotton or six strands floss and backstitch, embroider letters on F as indicated on graph.

NOTE: Cut raffia in half.
3: Thread each end of one raffia length through

one cutout on Wall Hanging; tie into a bow. Tie remaining raffia into a bow around Door Hanger handle as shown in photo. Glue Sunflower, Leaves, Stem and Pot to Wall Hanging as shown in photo.

—*Designed by Michele Wilcox*

B – Sunflower
(20w x 20h-hole piece)
Cut 1 & work.

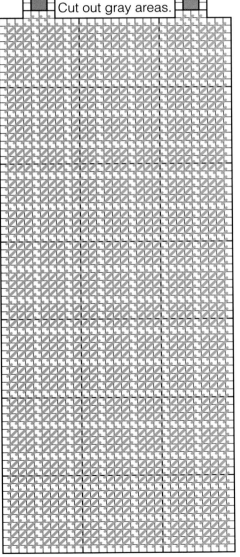

COLOR KEY: In My Garden

No. 3 pearl cotton or floss	AMOUNT
■ Black	3 yds. [2.7m]

Worsted-weight	YARN AMOUNT
Baby Blue	32 yds. [29.3m]
Eggshell	20 yds. [18.3m]
Holly	9 yds. [8.2m]
Rust	8 yds. [7.3m]
Yellow	6 yds. [5.5m]
Brown	2 yds. [1.8m]
Gold	1 yd. [0.9m]
Cinnamon	¼ yd. [0.2m]

STITCH KEY:
━ Backstitch/Straight

E – Pot
(25w x 21h-hole piece)
Cut 1 & work.

A – Wall Hanging Back
(29w x 73h-hole piece)
Cut 1 & work.

Cut out gray areas.

F – Door Hanger
(35w x 57h-hole piece)
Cut 1 & work.

Cut Out

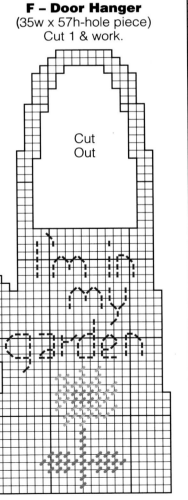

C – Leaf
(12w x 7h-hole pieces)
Cut 4 & work.

WILDFLOWER FABRIC PILLOWS

Outstanding wildflower pillows add charm and
a fresh look to any room, from your sunporch to the den.

SIZE
13¾" x 14¼" [35cm x 36.2cm].

SKILL LEVEL: Challenging

MATERIALS FOR ONE OF EACH
- Four sheets of 5-mesh plastic canvas
- Two 14" [35.6cm] pillow forms
- Sewing needle and matching-color quilting thread

- 44"-wide [111.8cm] cotton fabric; for amounts see individual Color Keys.

FABRIC PREPARATION INSTRUCTIONS
1: If desired, prewash in cool water.

2: For fabric strips, measuring along one selvage edge of fabric, mark every ¾" [19mm] and snip with sharp scissors to begin tear.

3: Holding fabric firmly with both hands, starting at cut, tear into strips. Discard first and last strips if not correct width. Remove any long threads from strips.

CUTTING INSTRUCTIONS
A: For Poinsettia Front and Back, cut two (one for Front and one for Back) 70w x 66h-holes.
B: For Sunflower Front and Back, cut two (one for Front and one for Back) 70w x 66h-holes.
C: For Poinsettia Leaf Fronts and Backings, cut four (two for Fronts and Two for Backings) according to graph.
D: For Sunflower Leaf Fronts and Backings, cut four (two for Fronts and two for Backings) according to graph.

STITCHING INSTRUCTIONS
NOTES: One A, one B and two of each C and D pieces are not worked for Backings. To thread needle, fold one short end of strip in half and slide through eye of needle. Handle strips carefully to prevent excessive fraying.

1: Using colors and stitches indicated, work one A for Front, one B for Front (Leave uncoded areas of A and B pieces unworked.), one C for Front and one D for Front according to graphs.

2: Using green and straight stitch, embroider stems on Front A and Front B pieces as indicated on graphs. Using yellow and rya knot, embroider Poinsettia center as indicated.

NOTE: Cut black strips into 6" [15.2cm] lengths.

3: For Sunflower center, knot black strips to bars on unworked area of Front B to cover; trim ends.

4: For each Leaf, holding one unworked piece to wrong side of matching worked piece, with green, whipstitch together. Tack leaves to corresponding pillow fronts as shown in photo.

5: For each pillow, holding one back to wrong side of Front with one pillow form between, with floral print, whipstitch together.

—*Designed by Mary Craft*

COLOR KEY: Poinsettia

	44"-wide fabric	AMOUNT
	Blue	2 yds. [1.8m]
	Rose	1 yd. [0.9m]
	Green	1/3 yd. [0.3m]
	Floral print	1/4 yd. [0.2m]
	Red	1/4 yd. [0.2m]
	Yellow	1/4 yd. [0.2m]

STITCH KEY:

- Backstitch/Straight
- Rya Knot

A – Poinsettia Front & Back
(70w x 66h-hole pieces) Cut 1 each & work.

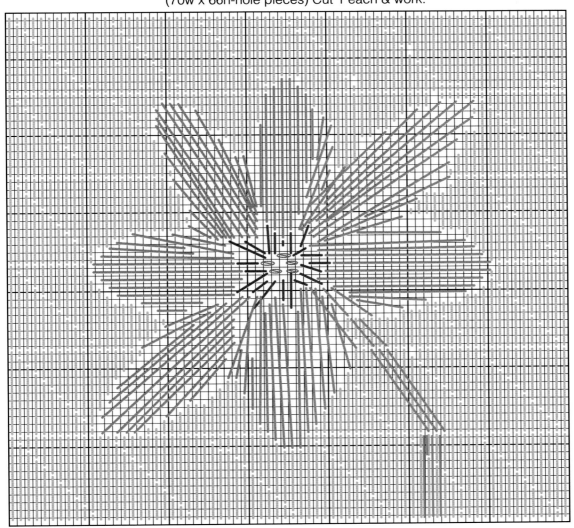

C – Poinsettia
Leaf Front & Backing
(22w x 18h-hole pieces)
Cut 4. Work 2 for Fronts &
leave 2 unworked for Backings.

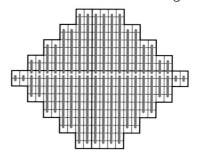

COLOR KEY: Poinsettia

44"-wide fabric		AMOUNT
	Blue	2 yds. [1.8m]
	Rose	1 yd. [0.9m]
	Green	1/3 yd. [0.3m]
	Floral print	1/4 yd. [0.2m]
	Red	1/4 yd. [0.2m]
	Yellow	1/4 yd. [0.2m]

COLOR KEY: Sunflower

44"-wide fabric		AMOUNT
	Blue	2 yds. [1.8m]
	Black	1 yd. [0.9m]
	Yellow	1 yd. [0.9m]
	Floral Print	1/2 yd. [0.5m]
	Green	1/3 yd. [0.3m]

STITCH KEY:
- Backstitch/Straight

D – Sunflower
Leaf Front & Backing
(8w x 27h-hole pieces)
Cut 4. Work 2 for Fronts &
leave 2 unworked for Backings.

B – Sunflower Front & Back
(70w x 66h-hole pieces) Cut 1 each & work.

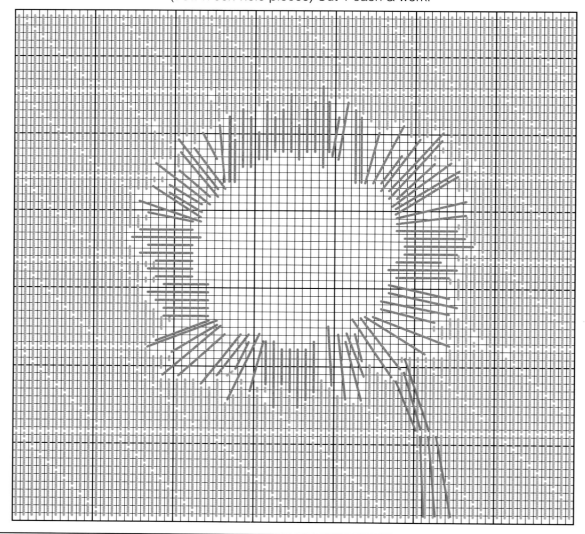

CHEERY SUNFLOWERS

Brighten your home, or a friend's day, with this uplifting sunflower set.

SIZES
Tissue Cover snugly covers a boutique-style tissue box; Utensil Caddy is 6" across x 6¼" tall [15.2cm x 15.9cm].

SKILL LEVEL: Average

MATERIALS
- One white 12" x 18" [30.5cm x 45.7cm] or larger sheet of 7-mesh plastic canvas
- Two standard-size sheets of light blue and one sheet of clear 7-mesh plastic canvas
- One Darice® 6" [15.2cm] plastic canvas circle
- Craft glue or glue gun
- Worsted-weight or plastic canvas yarn; for amounts see Color Key on page 46.

CUTTING INSTRUCTIONS
NOTE: Use light blue for A, B and F pieces, white for C and E pieces and clear canvas for remaining pieces.

A: For Tissue Cover Top, cut one according to graph.

B: For Tissue Cover Sides, cut four from light blue 30w x 36h-holes (no graph).

C: For Tissue Cover Fences, cut four according to graph.

D: For Utensil Caddy Bottom, use 6" circle (no graph).

E: For Utensil Caddy Horizontal Strips, cut seven from white 3w x 120h-holes (no graph).

F: For Utensil Caddy Vertical Strips, cut twenty-four from light blue 3w x 33h-holes (no graph).

G: For Sunflower Backs, cut two according to graph.

H: For Sunflower Petals #1 and #2, cut eight each according to graphs.

I: For Sunflower Centers, cut two according to graph.

J: For Sunflower Leaves #1 and #2, cut two each according to graphs.

STITCHING INSTRUCTIONS
NOTE: A-F pieces are not worked.

1: Using colors and stitches indicated, work G-J pieces according to graphs; with matching colors, overcast edges.

2: For each Sunflower (make 2), glue four H#1, four H#2 and one I to worked side of one G according to Sunflower Assembly Illustration on page 46. With white, whipstitch and assemble corresponding pieces according to individual assembly diagrams.

—Designed by Carolyn Christmas

A – Tissue Cover Top
(30w x 30h-hole piece)
Cut 1 from light blue & leave unworked.

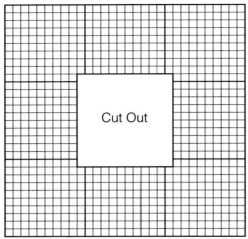

Sunflower Assembly Illustration
(Pieces are shown in different colors for contrast.)

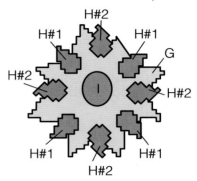

COLOR KEY: Cheery Sunflowers

Worsted-weight		YARN AMOUNT
	Yellow	29 yds. [26.5m]
	White	22 yds. [20.1m]
	Christmas Green	12 yds. [11m]
	Brown	6 yds. [5.5m]

STITCH KEY:
- ◉ French Knot

I – Sunflower Center
(13w x 13h-hole pieces)
Cut 2 from clear & work.

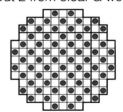

C – Tissue Cover Fence
(30w x 31h-hole pieces)
Cut 4 from white & leave unworked.
Cut out gray areas.

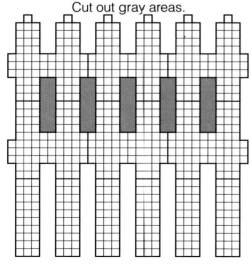

G – Sunflower Back
(34w x 34h-hole pieces)
Cut 2 from clear & work.

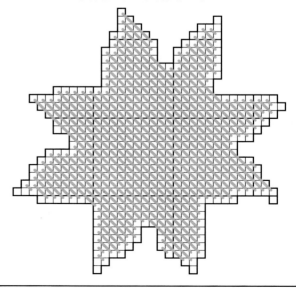

J – Sunflower Leaf #2
(14w x 17h-hole pieces)
Cut 2 from clear & work.

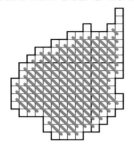

J – Sunflower Leaf #1
(14w x 17h-hole pieces)
Cut 2 from clear & work.

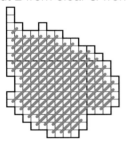

H – Sunflower Petal #2
(7w x 6h-hole pieces)
Cut 8 from clear & work.

H – Sunflower Petal #1
(7w x 6h-hole pieces)
Cut 8 from clear & work.

Tissue Cover Assembly Diagram
(Pieces are shown in different colors for contrast; gray denotes wrong side.)

Step 1:
Holding one C to each B, whipstitch A-C pieces together through all thicknesses.

Step 3:
Glue one Sunflower & one of each J to one side of Cover.

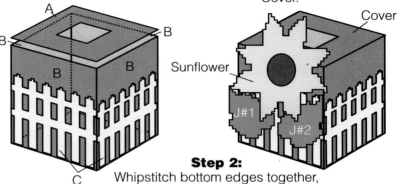

Step 2:
Whipstitch bottom edges together, overcasting unfinished edges of sides as you work.

Utensil Caddy Assembly Diagram
(Pieces are shown in different colors for contrast; gray denotes wrong side.)

Step 1:
Spacing each F (**NOTE:** Back pieces are shown in darker color for contrast.) two holes apart & weaving E pieces as you work, whipstitch D, top & bottom E & F pieces together.

Step 2:
Starting & ending at one F, weave remaining E pieces around Basket.

Step 3:
Spacing E pieces two holes apart between top & bottom pieces, using long stitch, whipstitch seams & F together.

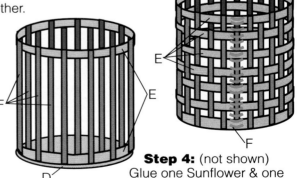

Step 4: (not shown)
Glue one Sunflower & one of each J to Basket.

ROSEBUDS & RIBBONS

*Soft and pleasing romance emanates from this
pretty and feminine basket, suitable for ladies of all ages.*

SIZE
7½" x 8¾" x about 10" tall [19cm x 22.2cm
x 25.4cm].

SKILL LEVEL: Average

MATERIALS
• Two sheets of 7-mesh plastic canvas
• 1½ yds. [1.4m] of white 1" [2.5cm] pregathered eyelet lace
• Craft glue or glue gun
• ¼" [6mm] satin ribbon; for amount see
  Color Key.
• Worsted-weight or plastic canvas yarn; for
  amounts see Color Key.

CUTTING INSTRUCTIONS
   A: For Side Pieces, cut two 87w x 34h-holes
(no graph).
   B: For Bottom, cut one according to graph.
   C: For Handle, cut two 56w x 6h-holes
(no graph).
   D: For Border Pieces, cut two 90w x 10h-
holes (no graph).

STITCHING INSTRUCTIONS
1: Overlapping two holes at each end of each
A and working through both thicknesses at
overlap areas to join, using colors indicated
and long stitch, work A pieces according to
Side Stitch Pattern Guide.

2: Overlapping six holes at one end of each C
and working through both thicknesses at overlap area to join, using lilac and long stitch,
work C pieces according to Handle Stitch
Pattern Guide.

3: Overlapping two holes at each end of each
D and working through both thicknesses at
overlap areas to join, using colors indicated
and continental stitch, work D pieces according to Border Stitch Pattern Guide. (*NOTE:
Pattern will not end evenly.)* For each blossom
on D pieces, thread ribbon from back to front
and then front to back through each ◆ hole as
indicated on Border Stitch Pattern Guide,
forming ½" [13mm] loop; glue loop to Border
as shown in photo.

4: With watermelon for long edges of Border
and lilac for Handle, overcast edges of C and
D pieces.

5: With lilac, whipstitch A and B pieces together, forming Basket; overcast unfinished edge.

NOTE: Cut lace in half.

6: Glue one lace piece to wrong side of each edge of Border as shown in photo. Glue each end of Handle to inside and Border to Basket as shown.

—Designed by Fran Rohus

Handle Stitch Pattern Guide

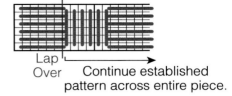

Lap Over

Continue established pattern across entire piece.

Side Stitch Pattern Guide

Lap Over

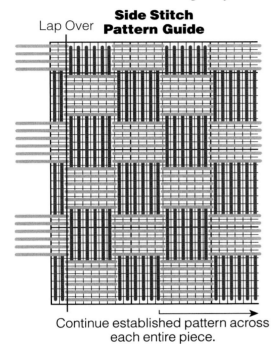

Continue established pattern across each entire piece.

Border Stitch Pattern Guide

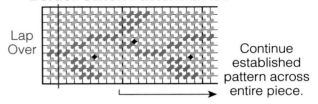

Lap Over

Continue established pattern across entire piece.

COLOR KEY: Rosebuds & Ribbons

1/4" ribbon	AMOUNT
☐ Purple	3 yds. [2.7m]

Worsted-weight	YARN AMOUNT
◼ Lilac	55 yds. [50.3m]
▨ Light Pink	45 yds. [41.1m]
▨ White	30 yds. [27.4m]
◼ Fern	9 yds. [8.2m]
☐ Watermelon	8 yds. [7.3m]

STITCH KEY:
✦ Ribbon Attachment

B – Bottom
(55w x 43-hole piece) Cut 1 & leave unworked.

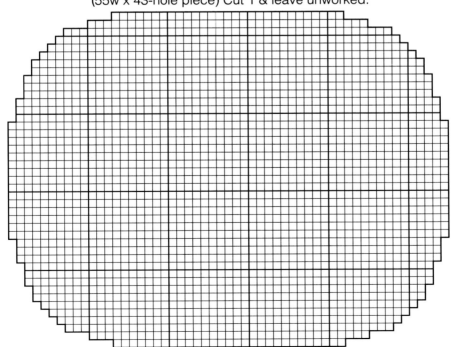

SEASONAL MESSAGES

*Declare a special meaning for every season
with this inspirational design you can display year-round.*

SIZE
Cross is 11⅛" x 15⅜" [28.3cm x 39.1cm].

SKILL LEVEL: Average

MATERIALS
- Two sheets of clear and one sheet of white 13½" x 21½" [34.3cm x 54.6cm] 7-mesh plastic canvas
- Twelve 2mm, seven 3mm and ten 5mm desired color round beads
- One white 9" x 12" [22.9cm x 30.5cm] sheet of felt
- Velcro® closure strips
- Craft glue or glue gun
- Worsted-weight or plastic canvas yarn; for amounts see Color Key on page 52.

CUTTING INSTRUCTIONS
NOTE: Use white for Backing A and clear canvas for remaining pieces.

A: For Cross Front and Backing, cut two (one from clear for front and one from white for Backing) according to graph.

B: For Message Bases, cut one each according to graphs.

C: For "Hope" Flowers, cut ten according to graph.

D: For "Hope" Leaves, cut ten according to graph.

E: For "Peace" Flowers, cut seven according to graph.

F: For "Peace" Leaves, cut ten according to graph.

G: For "Peace" Tendrils, cut six according to graph.

H: For "Faith" Flowers, cut twelve according to graph.

I: For "Faith" Leaves, cut eight according to graph.

J: For "Rejoice" Small Flower Petals, cut two according to graph.

K: For "Rejoice" Large Flower Petals, cut two according to graph.

L: For "Rejoice" Flower Centers, cut two according to graph.

M: For "Rejoice" Leaves, cut six according to graph.

N: For Message Backings, using B pieces as patterns, cut one each from felt ⅛" [3mm] smaller at all edges.

STITCHING INSTRUCTIONS
NOTES: One A for Backing is not worked.
For easier stitching and overcasting on smaller pieces of canvas, separate indicated color or colors of worsted-weight yarn into 2-ply or nylon plastic canvas yarn into 1-ply strands.

1: Using colors and stitches indicated, work one A for Front, B-F, H-K and M pieces according to graphs; fill in uncoded areas of B pieces using white and continental stitch. With pink for "Hope," bright blue for "Peace," tangerine for "Faith," and Christmas red for "Rejoice," overcast unfinished edges of B pieces; with yellow, overcast edges of L.

2: Using yellow and French knot, embroider detail on L pieces as indicated on graph. With fern for "Peace" Tendrils and with matching colors, overcast edges of C-K and M pieces.

3: Holding Backing A to wrong side of Front A, with white, whipstitch together.

4: Glue Flowers, Leaves and Tendrils to right side of B pieces as shown in photo and felt backing to wrong side of each corresponding Message Base. Glue 2mm beads to "Faith" Flowers, 3mm beads to "Peace" Flowers and 5mm beads to "Hope" Flowers as shown.

5: Glue two loopy-side Velcro closures to right side of Cross as indicated; glue two fuzzy-side closures to corresponding area on back of each Message Base. Hang as desired.

—Designed by Vicki Blizzard

A – Cross Front & Backing
(73w x 101h-hole pieces) Cut 1 from clear & work for Front.
Cut 1 from white & leave unworked for Backing.

J – "Rejoice" Small Flower Petals
(15w x 15h-hole pieces)
Cut 2 & work.

L – "Rejoice" Flower Center
(4w x 4h-hole pieces)
Cut 2 & work.

M – "Rejoice" Leaf
(5w x 8h-hole pieces)
Cut 6 & work.

K – "Rejoice" Large Flower Petals
(19w x 19h-hole pieces)
Cut 2 & work.

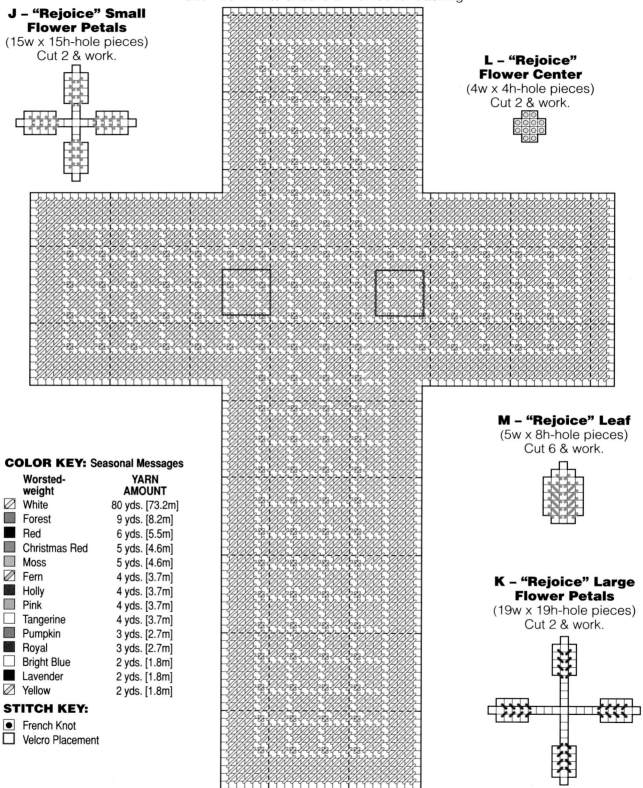

COLOR KEY: Seasonal Messages

Worsted-weight	YARN AMOUNT
White	80 yds. [73.2m]
Forest	9 yds. [8.2m]
Red	6 yds. [5.5m]
Christmas Red	5 yds. [4.6m]
Moss	5 yds. [4.6m]
Fern	4 yds. [3.7m]
Holly	4 yds. [3.7m]
Pink	4 yds. [3.7m]
Tangerine	4 yds. [3.7m]
Pumpkin	3 yds. [2.7m]
Royal	3 yds. [2.7m]
Bright Blue	2 yds. [1.8m]
Lavender	2 yds. [1.8m]
Yellow	2 yds. [1.8m]

STITCH KEY:
- ● French Knot
- ☐ Velcro Placement

H – "Faith" Flower
(3w x 3h-hole pieces)
Cut 12. Work 4; substituting tangerine for pumpkin, work 8.

I – "Faith" Leaf
(5w x 6h-hole pieces)
Cut 8 & work.

C – "Hope" Flower
(3w x 3h-hole pieces)
Cut 10 & work.

D – "Hope" Leaf
(5w x 7h-hole pieces)
Cut 10 & work.

E – "Peace" Flower
(3w x 3h-hole pieces)
Cut 7 & work.

F – "Peace" Leaf
(3w x 5h-hole pieces)
Cut 10 & work.

G – "Peace" Tendril
(4w x 4h-hole pieces)
Cut 6.

B – "Faith" Message Base
(37w x 14h-hole piece) Cut 1 & work.

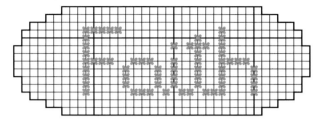

B – "Hope" Message Base
(38w x 18h-hole piece) Cut 1 & work.

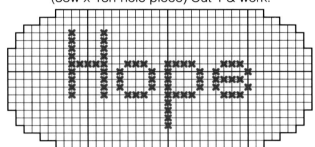

B – "Peace" Message Base
(43w x 14h-hole piece) Cut 1 & work.

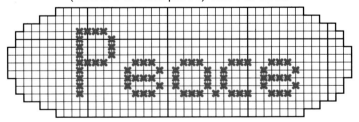

B – "Rejoice" Message Base
(47w x 15h-hole piece) Cut 1 & work.

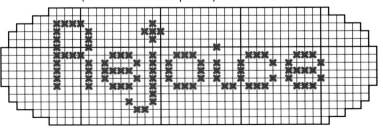

POT FULL OF PANSIES

Pretty pansies add a pleasing touch to
home furnishings with this artful planter or canister.

SIZES
Pot Cover is 5⅞" across x 5⅜" tall [15cm x 13.7cm]; Plant Poke is 3" x 3¼" [7.6cm x 8.2cm].

SKILL LEVEL: Average

MATERIALS
- One 12" x 18" [30.5cm x 45.7cm] or larger sheet of 7-mesh plastic canvas
- One Darice® 6" [15.2cm] plastic canvas circle
- 18" [45.7cm] length of floral wire
- Scrap of coordinating color felt

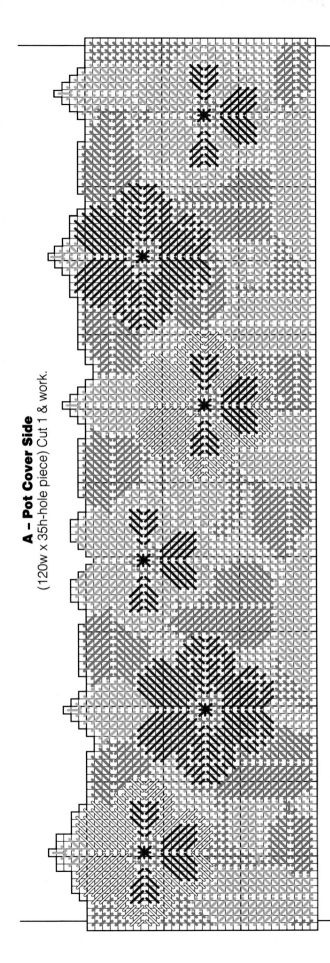

A – Pot Cover Side
(120w x 35h-hole piece) Cut 1 & work.

- Craft glue or glue gun
- Worsted-weight or plastic canvas yarn; for amounts see Color Key.

CUTTING INSTRUCTIONS

A: For Pot Cover Side, cut one according to graph.

B: For Pot Cover Bottom, use 6" circle (no graph).

C: For Plant Poke, cut one according to graph.

D: For Plant Poke backing, using C as a pattern, cut one from felt ⅛" [3mm] smaller at all edges.

STITCHING INSTRUCTIONS

NOTES: Plant Poke may be stitched with desired colors. B is not worked.

1: Using colors and stitches indicated, work A and C pieces according to graphs. With matching colors, whipstitch short ends of A together; overcast top unfinished edges. With matching colors, whipstitch A and B pieces together, forming Pot Cover.

2: With matching color, overcast edges of Plant Poke. Fold floral wire in half and glue one end to wrong side of Plant Poke; glue D to wrong side of Plant Poke over wire.

—*Designed by Nancy Marshall*

COLOR KEY: Pot Full of Pansies

Worsted-weight	YARN AMOUNT
☐ Fern	18 yds. [16.5m]
☐ Forest	18 yds. [16.5m]
■ Red	8 yds. [7.3m]
☑ White	8 yds. [7.3m]
☐ Yellow	8 yds. [7.3m]
■ Purple	6 yds. [5.5m]
☐ Tangerine	1½ yds. [1.4m]

C – Plant Poke
(21w x 19h-hole piece)
Cut 1 & work.

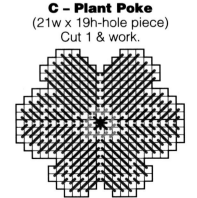

MINI FLORAL POTS

*These mini pots will inspire flights of floral fancy,
and make great holders for small plants or little gifts for loved ones.*

SIZE
Each is about 3" across x 3½" tall [7.6cm x 8.9cm], not including flowers.

SKILL LEVEL: Average

MATERIALS FOR ONE
- ¼ sheet of 7-mesh plastic canvas
- One 3" [7.6cm] plastic canvas radial circle
- ⅓ yd. [0.3m] of white ⅝" [16mm] satin ribbon (for Ribbon Trim)
- One ⅞" [2.2cm] metal or 1¾" [4.4cm] plastic ring
- Coordinating-color bouquet of artificial flowers with greenery
- 3" [7.6cm] Styrofoam® ball
- 12 oz. plastic cup
- Craft glue or glue gun
- Worsted-weight or plastic canvas yarn; for amounts see individual Color Keys.

CUTTING INSTRUCTIONS
   A: For Weaver Side, cut one 60w x 22h-holes.
   B: For Diamonds Side, cut one 61w x 21h-holes (no graph).
   C: For Ribbon Trim Side, cut one 61w x 22h-holes (no graph).
   D: For Bottom, use 3" circle (no graph).

WEAVER
STITCHING INSTRUCTIONS
NOTE: D is not worked.

1: Using sail blue and long stitch, work A according to graph. Using watermelon and running stitch, embroider detail as indicated on graph.

2: With sail blue, whipstitch short ends of A together. With watermelon, whipstitch side and D together, forming Basket; overcast

unfinished top edge, working over bars to fill in uncoded areas.

***NOTE:** Cut six 1-yd. [0.9m] lengths and one 12" 30.5cm] length of watermelon.*

3: For each cord, thread one 1-yd. strand of watermelon through neighboring ◆ holes as indicated on graph. Fold each strand in half; pull ends to even. Twist strands separately in same direction until tight; knot strands together to secure. (***NOTE:** When knotted, strands will twist together.)*

4: Untie knots and fold ends of each cord over metal or plastic ring about ¾" [19mm]. Wrap 12" strand around yarn just below ring to cover; knot and trim ends. Hide knot under yarn.

5: Glue foam ball inside bottom of cup; arrange flowers in foam. Place cup inside Basket.

DIAMONDS
STITCHING INSTRUCTIONS
NOTE: D is not worked.

1: Using sail blue and alternating scotch stitch over four bars, work B according to Diamonds Stitch Pattern Guide. Using watermelon and backstitch, embroider detail on B as indicated on Diamonds Stitch Pattern Guide.

2: With watermelon, whipstitch short ends of B together. Whipstitch side and D together, forming Basket; with sail blue, overcast unfinished top edges.

***NOTE:** Cut three 1-yd. [0.9m] lengths each of sail blue and watermelon and one 12" [30.5cm] length of watermelon.*

3: Substituting sail blue and watermelon for watermelon (*NOTE: Use one 1-yd. strand of each color for each cord.*) and using Weaver A graph as a guide for yarn attachments, follow Steps 3-5 of Weaver.

RIBBON TRIM
STITCHING INSTRUCTIONS
NOTE: D is not worked.

1: Using colors and stitches indicated, work C according to Ribbon Trim Stitch Pattern Guide. With sail blue, whipstitch short ends of C together. Whipstitch side and D together,

forming Basket; overcast unfinished top edge. *NOTE: Cut three 1-yd. [0.9m] lengths of sail blue and one 12" [30.5cm] length of watermelon.*

2: Substituting sail blue for watermelon (use 12" strand of watermelon to attach cords to ring) and using Weaver A graph as a guide for yarn attachments, follow Steps 3-5 of Weaver.

3: Starting at seam, weave ribbon under each motif as shown in photo; fold ends under and glue to Basket to secure.

—Designed by Catherine Bihlmaier

A – Weaver Side
(60w x 22h-hole piece) Cut 1 & work.

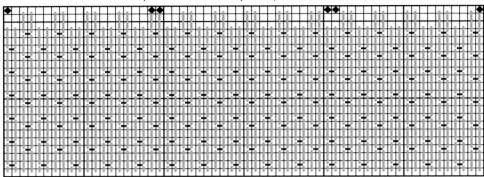

Ribbon Trim
Stitch Pattern Guide

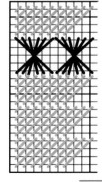

Continue established pattern
across entire piece.

Diamonds
Stitch Pattern Guide

Continue established pattern
across entire piece.

Chapter Three
SPEEDY SOUTHWEST

MAJESTIC WILDLIFE

Proudly display these exquisite portraits of Nature's majesty.

SIZE
Each is 11" x 14" [27.9cm x 35.6cm].

SKILL LEVEL: Average

MATERIALS
- Two 12" x 18" [30.5cm x 45.7cm] or larger sheets of 7-mesh plastic canvas
- Mat (optional) and frame of choice
- Worsted-weight or plastic canvas yarn; for amounts see individual Color Keys.

CUTTING INSTRUCTIONS
A: For Bighorn Sheep, cut one 73w x 93h-holes.
B: For Deer, cut one 73w x 93h-holes.

STITCHING INSTRUCTIONS
Using colors and stitches indicated, work pieces according to graphs; do not overcast. Frame as desired.

—Designed by Mike Clark

COLOR KEY: Bighorn Sheep

Worsted-weight	YARN AMOUNT
Sail Blue	19 yds. [17.4m]
Burgundy	15 yds. [13.7m]
Camel	9 yds. [8.2m]
Maple	8 yds. [7.3m]
Beige	7 yds. [6.4m]
Cinnamon	3 yds. [2.7m]
Sandstone	3 yds. [2.7m]
Eggshell	2 yds. [1.8m]
Black	1 yd. [0.9m]
White	1/4 yd. [0.2m]

A – Bighorn Sheep
(73w x 93h-hole piece)
Cut 1 & work.

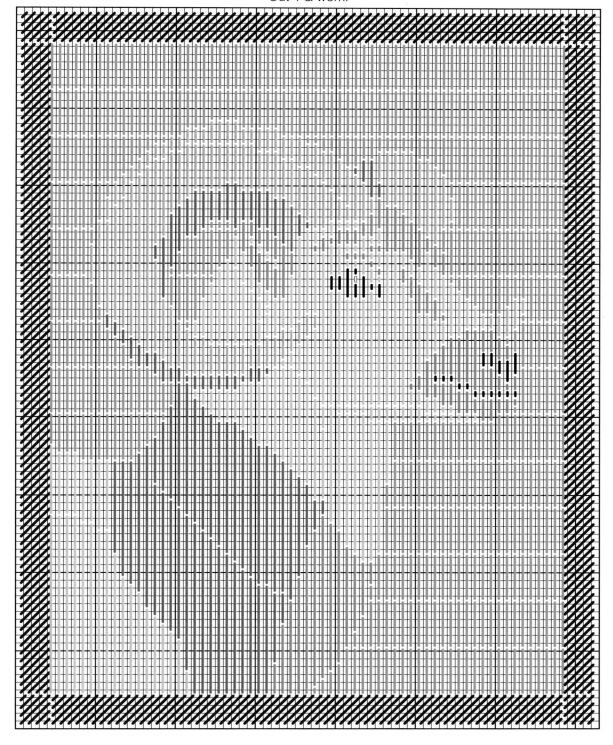

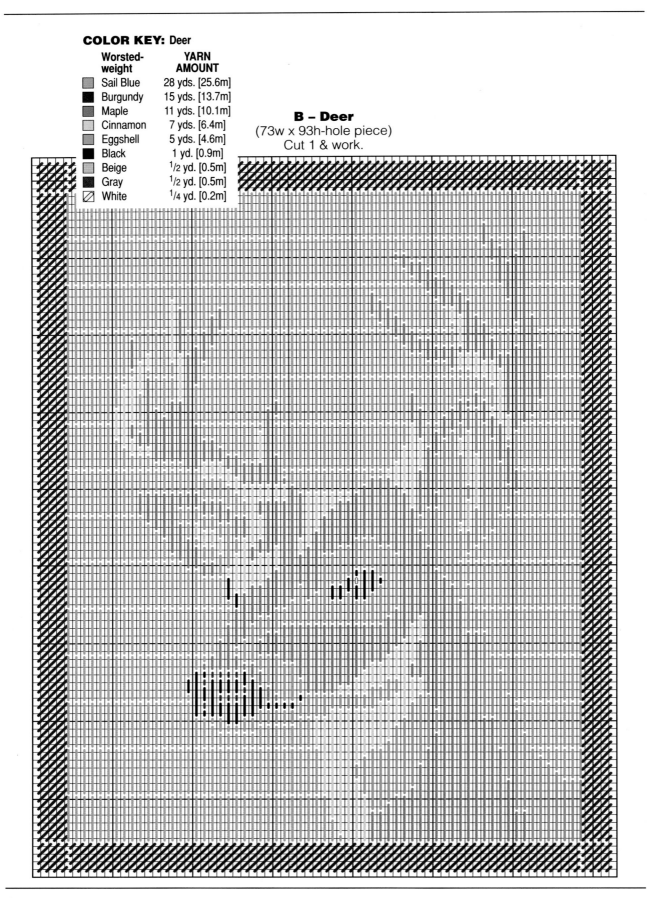

COLOR KEY: Deer

Worsted-weight		YARN AMOUNT
	Sail Blue	28 yds. [25.6m]
	Burgundy	15 yds. [13.7m]
	Maple	11 yds. [10.1m]
	Cinnamon	7 yds. [6.4m]
	Eggshell	5 yds. [4.6m]
	Black	1 yd. [0.9m]
	Beige	1/2 yd. [0.5m]
	Gray	1/2 yd. [0.5m]
	White	1/4 yd. [0.2m]

B – Deer
(73w x 93h-hole piece)
Cut 1 & work.

AZTEC WONDERS

Season your home decor with these dynamic accents fit for any room.

Cactus Window Screen

SIZE
8½" x 25" [21.6cm x 63.5cm].

SKILL LEVEL: Average

MATERIALS
• Two sheets of 7-mesh plastic canvas
• Four 9" x 12" [22.9cm x 30.5cm] sheets of gold felt (optional)
• Craft glue or glue gun
• Worsted-weight or plastic canvas yarn; for amounts see Color Key.

CUTTING INSTRUCTIONS
For Cactuses #1 and #2, cut two each according to graphs.

STITCHING INSTRUCTIONS
1: Using colors and stitches indicated, work pieces according to graphs.

NOTE: For optional backings, using one of each A and B pieces as a pattern, cut two each from felt ⅛" [3mm] smaller at all edges.

2: With rust, whipstitch pieces together as indicated and according to Screen Assembly Illustration (see photo); with matching colors, overcast unfinished edges. If desired, glue corresponding felt backings to wrong sides of A and B pieces.

—*Designed by Nancy Marshall*

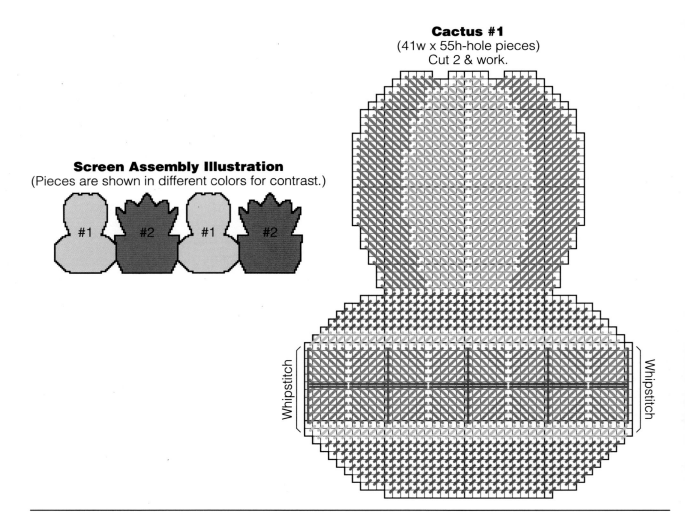

Cactus #1
(41w x 55h-hole pieces)
Cut 2 & work.

Screen Assembly Illustration
(Pieces are shown in different colors for contrast.)

#1 #2 #1 #2

Whipstitch

Whipstitch

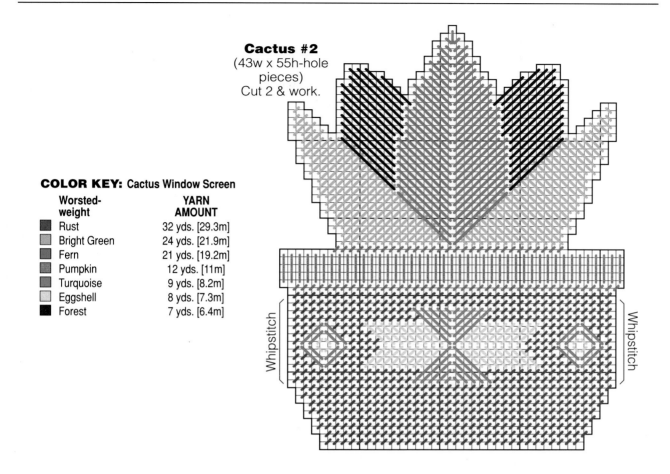

Cactus #2
(43w x 55h-hole pieces)
Cut 2 & work.

Whipstitch

Whipstitch

STARBURST PLACE MAT

SIZE
12" x 18" [30.5cm x 45.7cm], not including fringe.

SKILL LEVEL: Easy

MATERIALS
• One 12" x 18" [30.5cm x 45.7cm] or larger sheet of 7-mesh plastic canvas
• Worsted-weight or plastic canvas yarn; for amounts see Color Key on page 66.

CUTTING INSTRUCTIONS
For Starburst Place Mat, cut one 120w x 80h-holes.

STITCHING INSTRUCTIONS
1: Using colors and stitches indicated, work piece according to graph.

NOTE: Cut one hundred sixty 5" [12.7cm] lengths of pumpkin.

2: For fringe, attach one length with lark's head knot to each hole on short ends of piece (see photo); trim ends to even.

3: With matching colors, overcast unfinished edges.

—Designed by Marianne Telesca

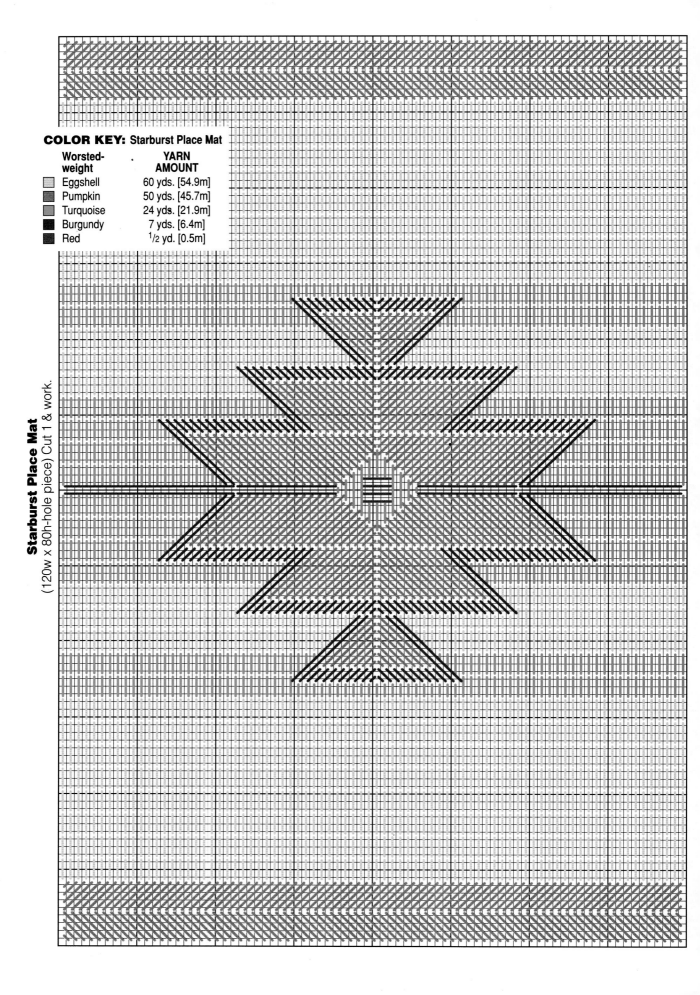

COLOR KEY: Starburst Place Mat

	Worsted-weight	.	YARN AMOUNT
	Eggshell		60 yds. [54.9m]
	Pumpkin		50 yds. [45.7m]
	Turquoise		24 yds. [21.9m]
	Burgundy		7 yds. [6.4m]
	Red		1/2 yd. [0.5m]

Starburst Place Mat
(120w x 80h-hole piece) Cut 1 & work.

WIND DANCER

The dancing feathers and beads on this
legendary bird entice every eye to look their way.

SIZE
10½" x 17½" [26.7cm x 44.5cm],
including feathers.

SKILL LEVEL: Average

MATERIALS
- Two black and one teal sheet of 7-mesh plastic canvas
- 23 silver 5mm round faceted beads
- Seven antique terra cotta and four antique light turquoise 10mm melon beads
- 11 antique silver 10.5mm corrugated rings
- Seven antique light turquoise and four antique terra cotta 16 x 12mm Moroccan beads
- 22 guinea feathers
- ⅛" [3mm] ribbon; for amount see Color Key on page 68.
- Worsted-weight or plastic canvas yarn; for amount see Color Key.

CUTTING INSTRUCTIONS
NOTE: Do not cut away hanger from black canvas sheets.

A: For Inner Bird Piece, cut one from teal according to graph.

B: For Outer Bird Pieces, cut two from black according to graph.

STITCHING INSTRUCTIONS
NOTE: Cut eleven 6" [15.2cm] lengths of ribbon.

1: For each dancer (make 11), using beads and rings in color combinations of choice (see photo), assemble one ribbon, two feathers, two faceted beads, one melon bead, one corrugated ring and one Moroccan bead according to Dancer Assembly Illustration on page 69; attach one dancer to each ◆ hole on A as indicated (see photo).

2: For eye, with ribbon, secure remaining faceted bead to cutout of A.

3: Holding B pieces together with A between and using bright orange and straight stitch,

work through all thicknesses according
to B graph.

4: Using remaining ribbon and running stitch,
work around outer row of holes of Bird
through all thicknesses to join.

—Designed by Sandra Miller Maxfield

COLOR KEY: Wind Dancer

¹/₈" ribbon	AMOUNT
☐ Black	8 yds. [7.3m]

Worsted-weight	YARN AMOUNT
▨ Bright Orange	1 yd. [0.9m]

STITCH KEY:
◈ Dancer Attachment

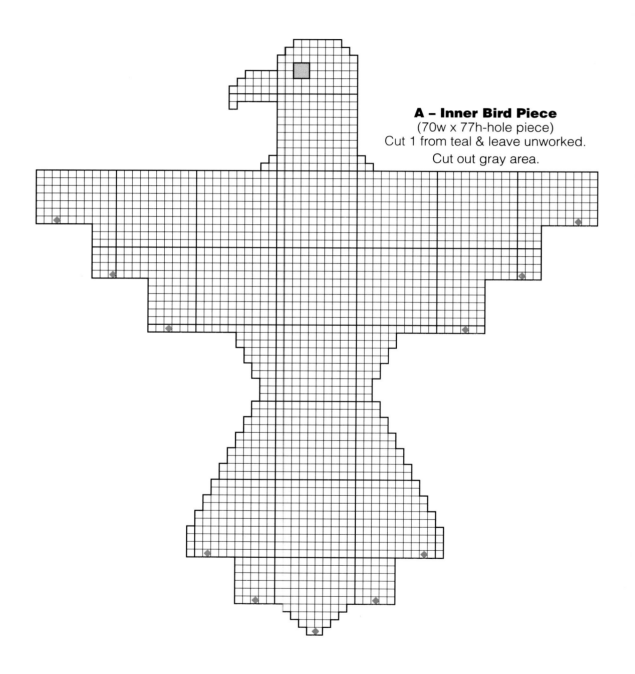

A – Inner Bird Piece
(70w x 77h-hole piece)
Cut 1 from teal & leave unworked.
Cut out gray area.

Dancer Assembly Illustration

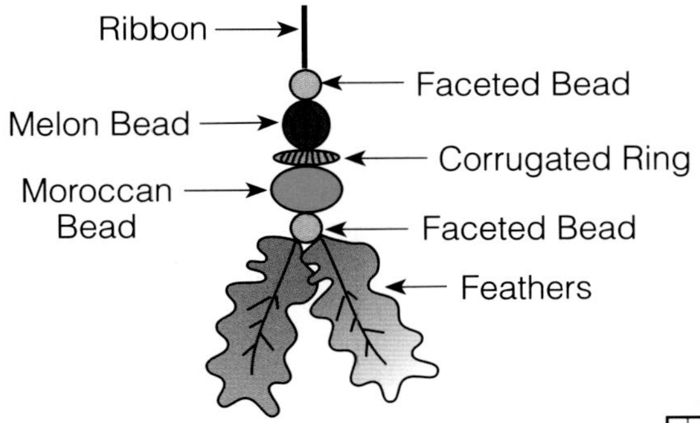

Ribbon

Faceted Bead

Melon Bead

Corrugated Ring

Moroccan Bead

Faceted Bead

Feathers

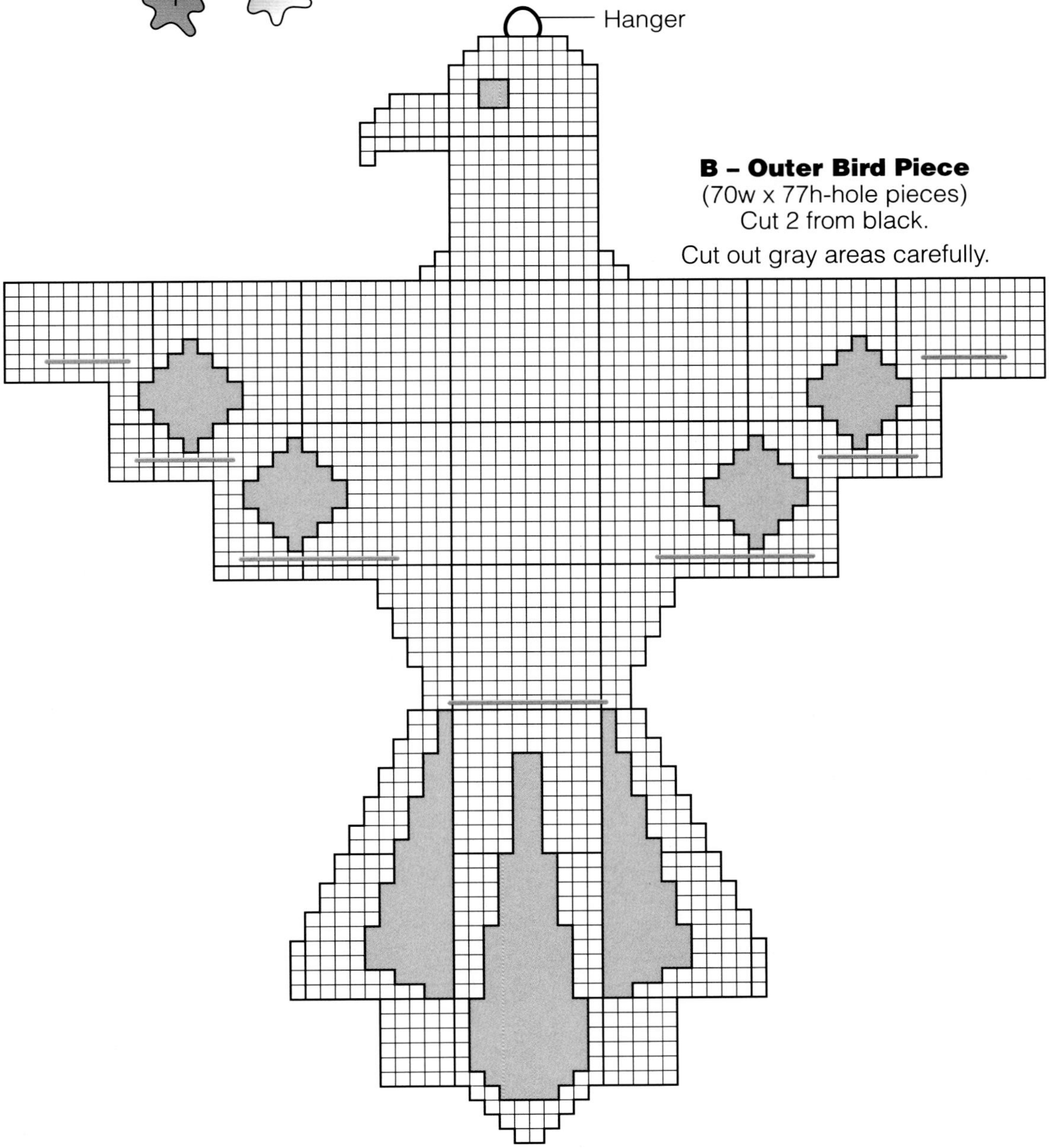

Hanger

B – Outer Bird Piece
(70w x 77h-hole pieces)
Cut 2 from black.

Cut out gray areas carefully.

TEPEE TREASURES

Send up sweet-smelling signals from
this inventive tepee, made to conceal an air freshener.

SIZE
4½" across x 6" tall [11.4cm x 15.2cm], not including dowels; conceals a Renuzit® air freshener.

SKILL LEVEL: Challenging

MATERIALS
- ½ sheet of 7-mesh plastic canvas
- One white 1½" x 1¾" [3.8cm x 4.4cm] ceramic cow skull
- One 1½" [3.8cm] antique-style concho
- Six small feathers
- Two small silver feather charms
- ⅔ yd. [0.6m] length of ⅛" [3mm] wooden dowel
- 12 or more each of light blue, yellow and white E beads
- Beading needle
- Six-strand embroidery floss; for amounts see Color Key.
- Worsted-weight or plastic canvas yarn; for amounts see Color Key.

CUTTING INSTRUCTIONS
A: For Front, cut one according to graph.
B: For Sides, cut five according to graph.

STITCHING INSTRUCTIONS
1: Using camel and stitches indicated, work pieces according to graphs.

2: Using dark brown and straight stitch, embroider door on A as indicated on graph.

3: With camel, whipstitch pieces wrong sides together as indicated, forming Tepee; overcast unfinished edges.

4: Using three strands floss in colors indicated and straight stitch and working over seam edges to achieve a continuous pattern, embroider remaining detail around Tepee as indicated.

NOTE: Cut dowel into six equal lengths; cut one 6" [15.2cm] length of camel.

5: Glue one end of each dowel inside one seam edge of Tepee 1½" [3.8cm] from top. Pull opposite ends of dowels together and wrap 6" strand of camel tightly around all dowels (see photo); secure ends of wraps.

NOTE: Cut six 1½" [3.8cm] lengths of yellow floss.

6: For each dancer (make 6), knot one end of each strand and thread two E beads of each color in order shown in photo onto each strand. Glue one feather inside bottom bead of each dancer. Secure opposite end of each dancer to one seam edge as shown.

7: With desired stitching material, attach one charm to each horn on cow skull. If desired, decorate concho with additional beads and floss. Glue skull and concho to Tepee as shown.

—*Designed by Mary Hill*

COLOR KEY: Tepee Treasures

Embroidery floss		AMOUNT
■	Blue	2 yds. [1.8m]
■	Yellow	2 yds. [1.8m]

Worsted-weight		YARN AMOUNT
■	Camel	36 yds. [32.9m]
■	Dk. Brown	2 yds. [1.8m]

STITCH KEY:

⊟ Backstitch/Straight

A – Front
(13w x 40h-hole piece)
Cut 1 & work.

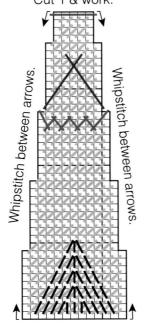

B – Side
(13w x 40h-hole pieces)
Cut 5 & work.

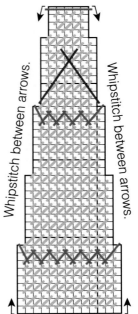

SOUTHWEST CELEBRATIONS

Captivating Kokopelli and ceremonial
figures kindle celebration wherever they are.

KOKOPELLI STATUE

SIZE
3" x 5½" x 10½" tall [7.6cm x 14cm x 26.7cm].

SKILL LEVEL: Easy

MATERIALS
- 1½ sheets of 7-mesh plastic canvas
- Zip-close bag filled with aquarium gravel or other weighting material
- Worsted-weight or plastic canvas yarn; for amounts see Color Key.

CUTTING INSTRUCTIONS
A: For Kokopelli Sides, cut two according to graph.

B: For Base Sides, cut two 35w x 8h-holes (no graph).

C: For Base Ends, cut two 18w x 8h-holes.

D: For Base Top and Bottom, cut two (one for Top and one for Bottom) 35w x 18h-holes (no bottom graph).

STITCHING INSTRUCTIONS
NOTE: Bottom D is not worked.

1: Using colors and stitches indicated, work A,

C and one D for top (leave indicated area unworked) pieces according to graphs; using turquoise and slanted gobelin stitch over narrow width, work B pieces.

2: Holding A pieces wrong sides together, with black, whipstitch together and to right side of Top D as indicated.

3: For Base, whipstitch B-D pieces together, inserting weighting material before closing.

—Designed by Mike Clark

A – Kokopelli Side
(36w x 62h-hole pieces)
Cut 2. Work 1 & 1 reversed.

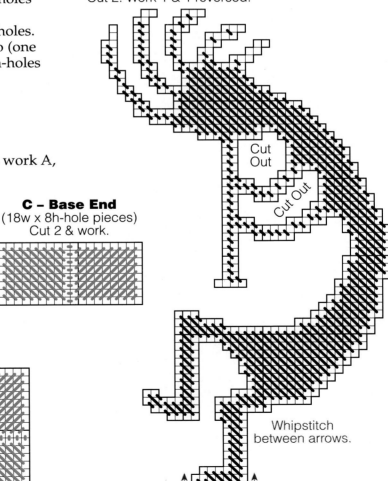

COLOR KEY: Kokopelli Statue

Worsted-weight	YARN AMOUNT
■ Black	16 yds. [14.6m]
▦ Turquoise	14 yds. [12.8m]

ATTACHMENT KEY:
☐ Kokopelli

C – Base End
(18w x 8h-hole pieces)
Cut 2 & work.

D – Base Top
(35w x 18h-hole piece)
Cut 1 & work.

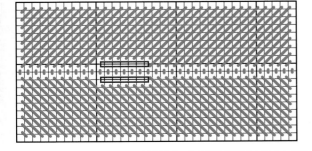

INDIAN CEREMONY

SIZE
Snugly covers a boutique-style tissue box.

SKILL LEVEL: Easy

MATERIALS
- 1½ sheets of 7-mesh plastic canvas
- Worsted-weight or plastic canvas yarn; for amounts see Color Key.

CUTTING INSTRUCTIONS
A: For Sides, cut four 30w x 36h-holes.
B: For Top, cut one according to graph.

STITCHING INSTRUCTIONS
1: Using colors and stitches indicated, work pieces according to graphs; with eggshell, overcast cutout edges of B.

2: With eggshell, whipstitch A and B pieces wrong sides together, forming Cover; overcast unfinished edges.

—Designed by Carolyn Christmas

COLOR KEY: Indian Ceremony

	Worsted-weight	YARN AMOUNT
	Eggshell	30 yds. [27.4m]
	Black	8 yds. [7.3m]
	Gray	8 yds. [7.3m]
	Peach	8 yds. [7.3m]
	Turquoise	8 yds. [7.3m]
	Brown	4 yds. [3.7m]
	Maple	4 yds. [3.7m]
	Rust	4 yds. [3.7m]

A – Side
(30w x 36h-hole pieces)
Cut 4 & work.

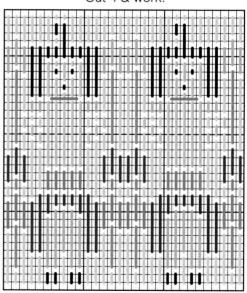

B – Top
(cut 1) 30 x 30 holes

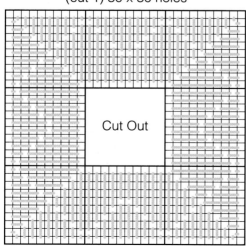

Cut Out

RED HOT FANS

Send messages of warmth and splendor with these fascinating fans.

SIZE
Each Fan is 1" x 11¼" x about 15¾" tall [2.5cm x 28.6cm x 40cm].

SKILL LEVEL: Challenging

MATERIALS
- One sheet each of light green and peach 7-mesh plastic canvas
- 6 yds. [5.5m] of light green and 3 yds. [2.7m] each of dark green, peach and off-white ¼" [6mm] picot-edged satin ribbon
- Two peach ½" x ¾" [13mm x 19mm] artificial rosebuds with leaves
- 20 peach ¼" [6mm] satin ribbon roses
- Craft glue or glue gun
- Worsted-weight or plastic canvas yarn; for amounts see Color Key on page 76.

CUTTING INSTRUCTIONS
A: For Fan Pieces, cut forty (twenty from light green and twenty from peach) according to graph.

B: For Urns #1 and #2, cut one each from clear according to graphs.

C: For Peppers #1 and #2, cut six each from clear according to graphs.

STITCHING INSTRUCTIONS
1: Using colors and stitches indicated and leaving uncoded areas unworked, work light green A, B and C pieces according to graphs; substituting aqua for forest, work peach A pieces according to graph. With matching colors, overcast edges of B and C pieces.

2: Using colors and embroidery stitches indicated, embroider detail on B pieces as indicated on graphs.

3: With forest for light green Fan and aqua for peach Fan, whipstitch and assemble corre-

sponding A pieces as indicated and according to Fan Assembly Diagram. Glue Urn #1 to light green Fan and Urn #2 to peach Fan as shown in photo.

NOTE: Cut ribbons into 1-yd. [0.9m] lengths.

4: Holding three light green and three dark green ribbons together as one, tie into a bow; repeat with remaining ribbons. Glue green bow to bottom of light green Fan and multi-color bow to bottom of peach Fan as shown; glue one rosebud to center of each bow. Glue one ribbon rose to every other Fan Piece (see photo).

5: For each Pepper group (make 4), glue three Peppers together as shown; glue one Pepper group to each of two bow tails on each Fan as shown. Hang or display as desired.

—Designed by Mary Lumpkin

C – Pepper #1
(9w x 20h-hole pieces)
Cut 6 from clear & work.

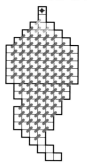

C – Pepper #2
(9w x 20h-hole pieces)
Cut 6 from clear & work.

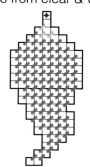

Fan Assembly Diagram
Step 1:
Whipstitch long edges of A pieces together; overcast unfinished long edges.

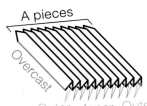

A pieces

Overcast

Outer Pair   Inner Pairs   Outer Pair

Step 2:
Fan fold & whipstitch bottom edges of each inner pair together (**NOTE:** There are eight individual inner pairs.)

Step 3:
Whipstitch bottom edges of outer pairs together through all thicknesses.

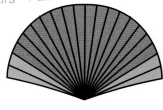

A – Fan Piece
(6w x 44h-hole pieces)
Cut 20 each from light green & peach; work.

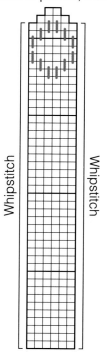

Whipstitch

Whipstitch

Whipstitch

B – Urn #2
(18w x 21h-hole piece)
Cut 1 from clear & work.

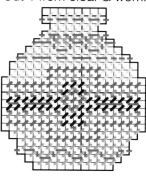

B – Urn #1
(23w x 21h-hole piece)
Cut 1 from clear & work.

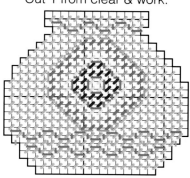

COLOR KEY: Red Hot Fans

Worsted-weight	YARN AMOUNT
Forest	58 yds. [53m]
Aqua	30 yds. [27.4m]
Dk. Orange	10 yds. [9.1m]
Flesh	3 yds. [2.7m]
Eggshell	2½ yds. [2.3m]

STITCH KEY:
⊟ Backstitch/Straight

ATTACHMENT KEY:
✦ Ribbon

BASIC VASE

*Decorate your home with the artistic lines
and sensuous color of this elegant and functional vase.*

SIZE
5" across x 4" tall [12.7cm x 10.2cm].

SKILL LEVEL: Easy

MATERIALS
- One sheet of 7-mesh plastic canvas
- Four brown and two opalescent blue 8mm pony beads
- Two small rust craft feathers
- One gold 1½" [3.8cm] round concho
- ⅓ yd. [0.3m] tan ⅛" [3mm] suede lacing
- Craft glue or glue gun
- Worsted-weight or plastic canvas yarn; for amounts see Color Key.

CUTTING INSTRUCTIONS
A: For Sides, cut four according to graph.
B: For Bottom, cut one 16w x 16h-holes (no graph).

STITCHING INSTRUCTIONS
NOTE: B is not worked.

1: Using colors and stitches indicated, work A pieces according to graph.

2: With turquoise, whipstitch A and B pieces together according to Vase Assembly Illustration; overcast unfinished edges.

3: Thread one end of lacing through each hole

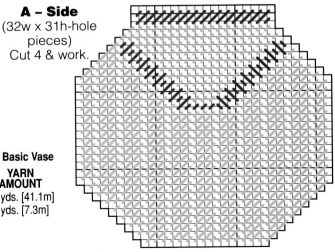

from back to front on concho; pull ends to even and tie around center of concho (see photo). Thread beads on each end of lacing in order shown in photo; knot each end of lacing to secure.

4: Glue feathers to wrong side of concho as shown; glue concho to one Vase Side.

—Designed by Lynn Lambert

Vase Assembly Illustration
(Gray denotes wrong side.)

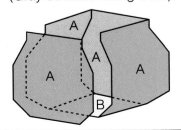

A – Side
(32w x 31h-hole pieces)
Cut 4 & work.

COLOR KEY: Basic Vase

Worsted-weight		YARN AMOUNT
☐	Turquoise	45 yds. [41.1m]
■	Rust	8 yds. [7.3m]

WESTERN FLAIR

*Give some western flavor to your
loved ones with these quick-to-stitch projects*

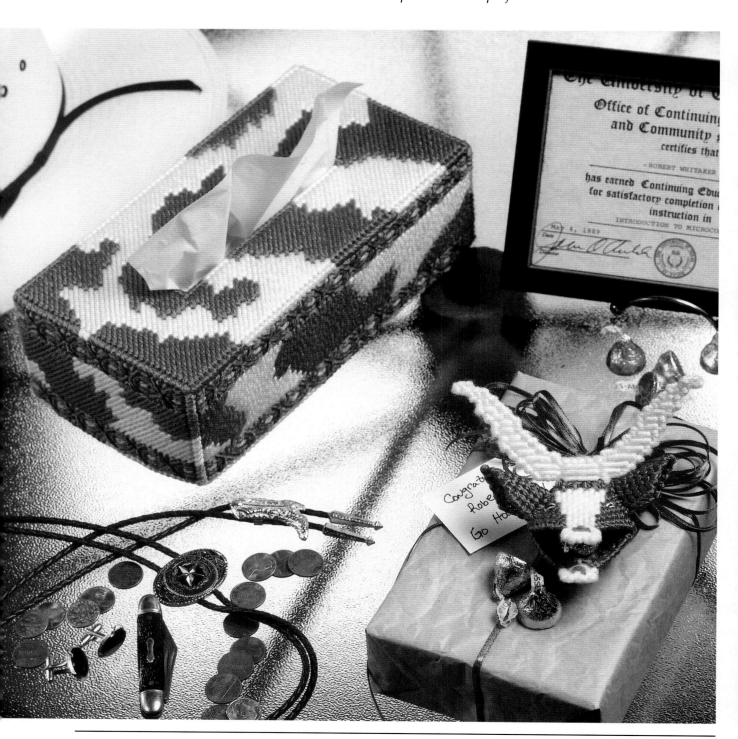

PINTO PATCHES

SIZE
Covers a 3⅛" x 4¾" x 9½" [7.9cm x 12.1cm x 24.1cm] tissue box.

SKILL LEVEL: Average

MATERIALS
- 1½ sheets of 7-mesh plastic canvas
- Worsted-weight or plastic canvas yarn; for amounts see Color Key.

CUTTING INSTRUCTIONS
A: For Sides, cut two 63w x 20h-holes.
B: For Ends, cut two 33w x 20h-holes.
C: For Top, cut one according to graph.

STITCHING INSTRUCTIONS
1: Using colors and stitches indicated, work pieces according to graphs; with matching colors, overcast cutout edges of C.

2: With matching colors as shown in photo and holding one of each A and B upside down so that pattern continues across corners, whipstitch A-C pieces wrong sides together; overcast unfinished edges.

—Designed by Carolyn Christmas

B – End (33w x 20h-hole pieces) Cut 2 & work.

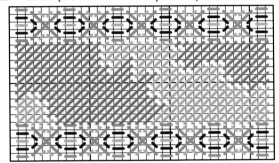

A – Side (63w x 20h-hole pieces) Cut 2 & work.

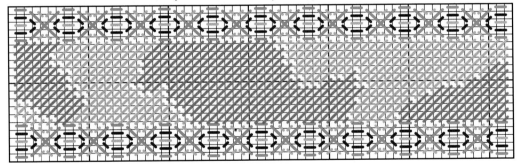

C – Top (63w x 33h-hole piece) Cut 1 & work.

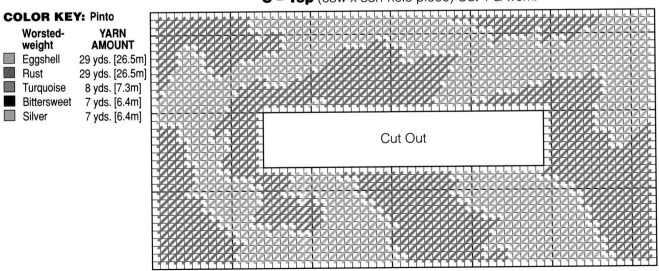

Cut Out

COLOR KEY: Pinto		
Worsted-weight		**YARN AMOUNT**
	Eggshell	29 yds. [26.5m]
	Rust	29 yds. [26.5m]
	Turquoise	8 yds. [7.3m]
	Bittersweet	7 yds. [6.4m]
	Silver	7 yds. [6.4m]

LONGHORN KISSY COW

SIZE
2¼" x 4" x 5" [5.7cm x 10.2cm x 12.7cm].

SKILL LEVEL: Challenging

MATERIALS
- ½ sheet of 7-mesh plastic canvas
- Six-strand embroidery floss; for amounts see Color Key.
- Worsted-weight or plastic canvas yarn; for amounts see Color Key.

CUTTING INSTRUCTIONS
A: For Top, cut one according to graph.
B: For Bottom, cut one according to graph.
C: For Back, cut one according to graph.
D: For Ears, cut two according to graph.
E: For Horns, cut one according to graph.

STITCHING INSTRUCTIONS
1: Using colors and stitches indicated, work pieces according to graphs. Omitting attachment edges, with matching colors, overcast edges of A, B, D and E pieces.

2: Using six strands floss in colors and embroidery stitches indicated, embroider eye detail on A as indicated on graph.

3: For each ear (make 2), fold one D wrong sides together as indicated and with rust, whipstitch Y edges together.

4: With rust, whipstitch A-C pieces wrong sides together as indicated, attaching D and E pieces to assembly as indicated as you work.

—*Designed by Della Johnson*

COLOR KEY: Longhorn Kissy Cow

Embroidery floss	AMOUNT
■ Black	¼ yd. [0.2m]
■ White	¼ yd. [0.2m]

Worsted-weight	YARN AMOUNT
■ Rust	6 yds. [5.5m]
■ Eggshell	3 yds. [2.7m]
■ White	2 yds. [1.8m]
■ Camel	1 yd. [0.9m]

STITCH KEY:
⊟ Backstitch/Straight

ATTACHMENT KEY:
☐ Ear
☐ Horns

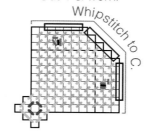

A – Top
(13w x 13h-hole piece)
Cut 1 & work.

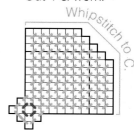

B – Bottom
(13w x 13h-hole piece)
Cut 1 & work.

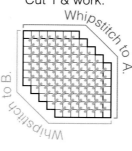

C – Back
(11w x 11h-hole piece)
Cut 1 & work.

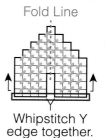

D – Ear
(9w x 9h-hole pieces)
Cut 2 & work.
Overcast between arrows.

Fold Line

Whipstitch Y edge together.

E – Horns
(32w x 14h-hole piece)
Cut 1 & work.
Overcast between arrows.

FAST
FAMILY FAVORITES

FLORAL PURSE MATES

Stay in style with these coordinated trimmings that keep everything neat and handy.

SIZES

Tissue Holder is 1⅛" x 2⅝" x 4¾" [2.9cm x 6.7cm x 12.1cm] and holds Kleenex® Pocket Pack tissues; Business Card Case is ¾" x 2⅝" x 4¼" [1.9cm x 6.7cm x 10.5cm]; Notebook Cover is ¾" x 3½" x 5⅜" [1.9cm x 8.9cm x 13.7cm] and covers a 3" x 5" [7.6cm x 12.7cm] side-opening spiral memo book; Checkbook Cover is ¾" x 3½" x 6½" [1.9cm x 8.9cm x 16.5cm]; Address Book Cover is ½" x 4" x 6½" [1.3cm x 10.2cm x 16.5cm].

SKILL LEVEL: Challenging

MATERIALS

- Three sheets of 10-mesh plastic canvas
- One gold purse clasp
- Two white ½" [6mm] self-stick Velcro® closures
- Six-strand embroidery floss; for amounts see Color Key.
- Baby or sport-weight yarn; for amount see Color Key.

CUTTING INSTRUCTIONS

A: For Tissue Holder Top, cut one according to graph.

B: For Tissue Holder Bottom, cut one 46w x 25h-holes (no graph).

C: For Tissue Holder Sides, cut two 46w x 10h-holes (no graph).

D: For Tissue Holder End and Outer Flap, cut two (one for End and one for Outer Flap) 25w x 10h-holes (no graphs).

E: For Tissue Holder Inner Flap, cut one 25w x 8h-holes (no graph).

F: For Business Card Case Flap, cut one according to graph.

G: For Business Card Case Front, cut one according to graph.

H: For Business Card Case Back, cut one 40w x 25h-holes (no graph).

I: For Business Card Case Bottom, cut one 40w x 4h-holes (no graph).

J: For Business Card Case Sides, cut two according to graph.

K: For Business Card Case Top, cut one 40w x 6h-holes (no graph).

L: For Notebook Cover Front and Back, cut two (one for Front and one for Back) 34w x 52h-holes (no Back graph).

M: For Notebook Cover Spine, cut one 6w x 52h-holes (no graph).

N: For Notebook Cover Inside Flaps, cut two

15w x 52h-holes (no graph).

O: For Checkbook Cover Front and Back, cut two (one for Front and one for Back) 64w x 34h-holes (no Back graph).

P: For Checkbook Cover Spine, cut one 64w x 6h-holes (no graph).

Q: For Checkbook Cover Inside Flaps #1 and #2, cut one according to graph for #1 and one 64w x 20h-holes for #2 (no #2 graph).

R: For Address Book Cover Front and Back, cut two (one for Front and one for Back) 39w x 64h-holes (no Back graph).

S: For Address Book Cover Spine, cut one 4w x 64h-holes (no graph).

T: For Address Book Cover Inside Flaps, cut two 32w x 64h-holes (no graph).

U: For Address Book Cover Stamp Pocket, cut one 15w x 35h-holes (no graph).

STITCHING INSTRUCTIONS
NOTES E, N, Q, T and U pieces are not worked. Use 12 strands embroidery floss.

1: Using colors and stitches indicated, work A, F, G, J and one of each L, O and R pieces for Fronts according to graphs; work B-D, H, I, K, remaining L for Back, M, remaining O for Back, P, remaining R for Back and S pieces according to background pattern established on A. (***NOTE:*** *Pattern will not end evenly on some pieces.*) With white, overcast cutout edges of A.

2: With white, whipstitch corresponding pieces together according to individual assembly diagrams on pages 83-85.

3: For Business Card Case, insert prongs on small clasp through holes to back of G; bend on wrong side to secure. Aligning prongs of large clasp to cutouts on Flap, slide clasp over unworked area of F (see photo); press clasp together to secure.

—Designed by Kathleen J. Fischer

Checkbook Cover Assembly Diagram
(inside view)

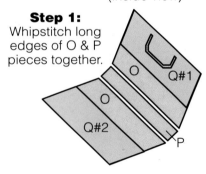

Step 1:
Whipstitch long edges of O & P pieces together.

Step 2:
Whipstitch O & Q pieces together at matching outer edges; overcast unfinished edges of O & P pieces.

F – Business Card Case Flap
(40w x 19h-hole piece) Cut 1 & work.
Whipstitch to K.

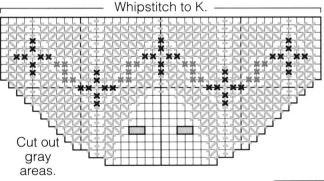

Cut out gray areas.

A – Tissue Holder Top
(46w x 25h-hole piece) Cut 1 & work.

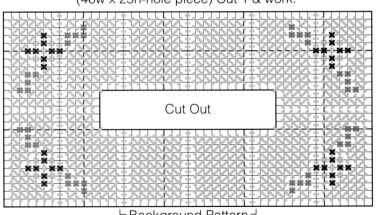

Cut Out

└ Background Pattern ┘

G – Business Card Case Front
(40w x 24h-hole piece)
Cut 1 & work.

Cut out gray areas.

Address Book Cover Assembly Diagram
(inside view)

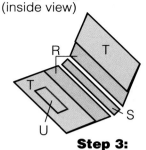

Step 1:
Whipstitch long edges of R & S pieces together.

Step 2:
Whipstitch short & one long end of U to center of one T.

Step 3:
With pocket opening on flap facing to inside, whipstitch R & T pieces together at matching outside edges.

Step 4:
Overcast unfinished edges.

COLOR KEY: Floral Purse Mates

Embroidery floss	AMOUNT
Med. Cobalt Blue	20 yds. [18.3m]
Med. Juniper	20 yds. [18.3m]
Med. Lt. Cobalt Blue	20 yds. [18.3m]
Med. Jonquil	8 yds. [7.3m]

Baby Yarn	AMOUNT
White	4¹/₂ oz. [127.6g]

J – Business Card Case Side
(4w x 25h-hole pieces)
Cut 2. Work 1 & 1 reversed.

O – Checkbook Cover Front
(64w x 34h-hole piece) Cut 1 & work.

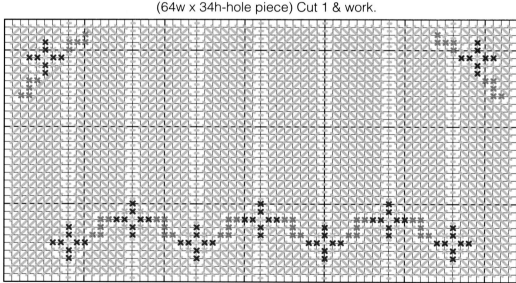

Q – Checkbook Cover Inside Flap #1
(64w x 20h-hole piece) Cut 1 & work.

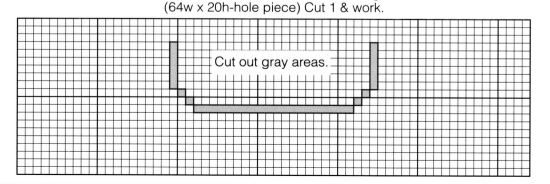

Cut out gray areas.

Tissue Holder Assembly Diagram

(Pieces are shown in different colors for contrast; gray denotes wrong side.)

Step 1:
Whipstitch one D to one end of A for Outer Flap, & E to one end of B.

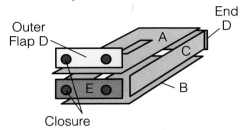

Step 2:
Whipstitch A-C & end D pieces together; overcast unfinished edges.

Step 3:
Attach closure to wrong side of Flap D & E right side of pieces.

R – Address Book Cover Front
(39w x 64h-hole piece)
Cut 1 & work.

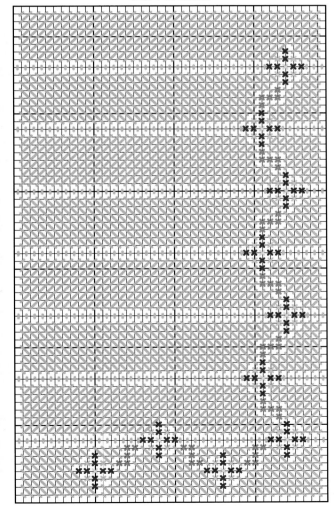

L – Notebook Cover Front
(34w x 52h-hole piece) Cut 1 & work.

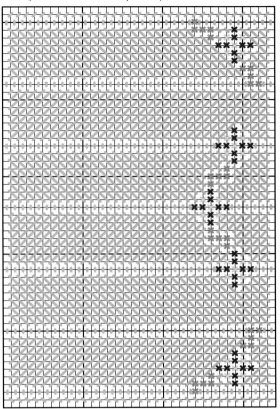

Business Card Case Assembly Diagram
(Gray denotes wrong side.)

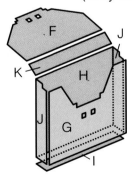

Step 1:
Whipstitch F-K pieces together.

Step 2:
Omitting cutout edges & purse clasp attachment area on flap, overcast unfinished edges.

Notebook Cover Assembly Diagram
(inside view)

Step 1:
Whipstitch long edges of L & M pieces together.

Step 2:
Whipstitch L & N pieces together at matching outside edges; overcast unfinished edges of L & M pieces.

PHEASANT DESK SET

Beset your desk with this fine set that is perfect for him or her.

SIZES

Box is 6¼" square x 2⅜" tall [15.9cm x 6cm], not including Pheasant; Pencil Box is 3¼" square x 4⅝" tall [8.3cm x 11.7cm]; Book Cover is ½" x 5½" x 9⅛" [1.3cm x 14cm x 23.1cm]; Desk Pad Holder is 17½" x 27" [44.5cm x 68.6cm], and holds 17" x 22" [43.2 x 55.9cm] sheets of paper.

SKILL LEVEL: Challenging

MATERIALS

• Three 12" x 18" [30.5cm x 45.7cm] or larger and three standard-size sheets of 7-mesh plastic canvas
• ½ sheet of 10-mesh plastic canvas
• Six-strand embroidery floss; for amount see Color Key on page 88.
• Heavy metallic braid or metallic cord; for amounts see Color Key.
• Worsted-weight or plastic canvas yarn; for amounts see Color Key.

CUTTING INSTRUCTIONS

NOTE: Use 10-mesh for E pieces, large sheets for L and M pieces and standard-size sheets of canvas for remaining pieces.

A: For Box Lid Top and Lining, cut two (one for Lid Top and one for Lining) 40w x 40h-holes.

B: For Box Lid Lip pieces, cut four 36w x 3h-holes (no graph).

C: For Box Sides, cut four 38w x 14h-holes (no graph).

D: For Box Bottom, cut one 38w x 38h-holes (no graph).

E: For Pheasant Sides, cut two from 10-mesh according to graph.

F: For Pheasant Base pieces, cut two according to graph.

G: For Pencil Box Sides, cut four 20w x 30h-holes.

H: For Pencil Box Bottom, cut one 20w x 20h-holes (no graph).

I: For Book Cover Front and Back, cut two (one for Front and one for Back) 36w x 60h-holes.

J: For Book Cover Spine, cut one 3w x 60h-holes (no graph).

K: For Book Cover Inside Flaps, cut two 30w x 60h-holes (no graph).

L: For Desk Pad Holder Back pieces, cut one from large sheet 80w x 116h-holes and two from large sheets 52w x 116h-holes (no graphs).

M: For Desk Pad Holder Flaps, cut two from large sheet 20w x 116h-holes (no graph).

STITCHING INSTRUCTIONS

NOTE: One A for Lining, B, D, H and K pieces are not worked.

1: For Box, using colors and stitches indicated, work one A and E pieces according to graphs. Fill in uncoded area of A using mermaid and E using brown and continental stitch. Using mermaid and slanted gobelin stitch over narrow width, work C pieces. Using eggshell and continental stitch, work F pieces; overcast unfinished edges.

2: With mermaid, whipstitch short ends of B pieces together, forming lid lip; whipstitch lid lip to Lining A as indicated on graph. Whipstitch A pieces together forming lid. Whipstitch B and C pieces together, forming box; overcast unfinished top edges.

3: With matching colors as shown in photo, whipstitch E pieces wrong sides together. Using six strands floss and modified turkey work and leaving 2" [5.1cm] loops, embroider grass at random on F pieces; cut loops and trim ends to desired lengths. Glue E and F pieces to lid top as indicated and as shown in photo.

4: For Pencil Box, using colors and stitches indicated, work G pieces according to graph.

With mermaid, whipstitch G and H pieces together; overcast unfinished edges.

5: For Book Cover, using colors and stitches indicated and stitching letter of choice to personalized (see Alphabet Graph), work I (omit letter on back) pieces according to graph. Using mermaid and slanted gobelin stitch over narrow width, work J. Whipstitch I-K pieces together according to Cover Assembly Diagram on page 89.

6: For Desk Pad Holder, using mermaid, and running stitch over three bars, overlapping

three holes at long edges of each L piece and working through both thicknesses at overlap areas to join, baste together (see Holder Assembly Diagram on page 88). Using mermaid and slanted gobelin stitch over three bars, work top and bottom edges of L and M pieces in horizontal row (see diagram); fill in uncoded areas of M pieces using striped pattern established on G.

7: With mermaid, whipstitch M pieces to matching outside edges of Holder Back (see diagram on page 88); overcast unfinished edges.

—Designed by Mike Clark

A – Box Lid Top & Lining
(40w x 40h-hole pieces) Cut 1 each from 7-mesh.
Work 1 for Lid Top & leave 1 unworked for Lining.

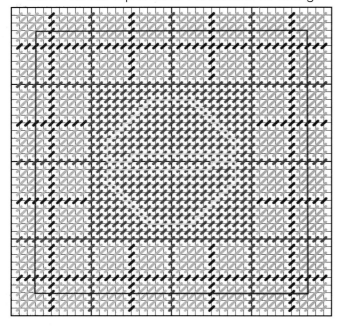

COLOR KEY: Pheasant Desk Set

Embroidery floss	AMOUNT
☐ Dk. Fudge	2 yds. [1.8m]

Metallic braid or cord	AMOUNT
◼ Beige	8 yds. [7.3m]
◼ Brown	8 yds. [7.3m]
◼ Black	2 yds. [1.8m]
◼ Green	2 yds. [1.8m]
◼ Orange	2 yds. [1.8m]
▨ White	2 yds. [1.8m]
◼ Lilac	1 yd. [0.9m]
◼ Red	1 yd. [0.9m]
◼ Star Yellow	1 yd. [0.9m]

Worsted-weight	YARN AMOUNT
◼ Eggshell	3 oz. [85.1g]
◼ Mermaid	2¹/₂ oz. [70.9g]
◼ Rust	60 yds. [54.9m]

OTHER:
☐ Lid Lip Attachment
☐ Pheasant Base /Box Lid Top Placement

Holder Assembly Illustration

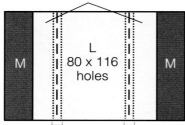

E – Pheasant Side
(58w x 34h-hole pieces)
Cut 2 from 10-mesh. Work 1 & 1 reversed.

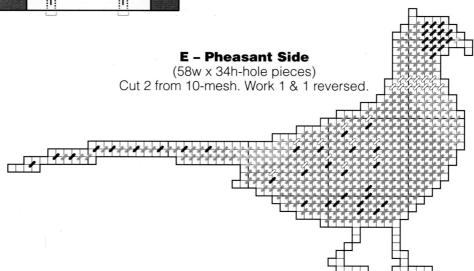

I – Book Cover Front & Back

(36w x 60h-hole pieces)
Cut 2 from 7-mesh. Work 1 for Front & 1 for Back.

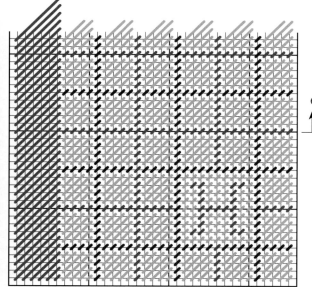

Continue
established
pattern
across
length of
piece.

F – Pheasant Base Piece

(16w x 8h-hole pieces)
Cut 2 from 7-mesh & work.

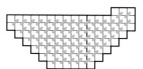

Cover Assembly Diagram

(Gray denotes wrong side.)

Step 1:
Holding I
pieces wrong
sides together
with J
between,
whipstitch
together.

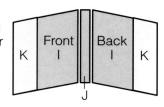

Step 2:
Holding K pieces to wrong side of Front & Back
at matching outside edges, whipstitch together
through all thicknesses; overcast unfinished
edges.

Alphabet Graph

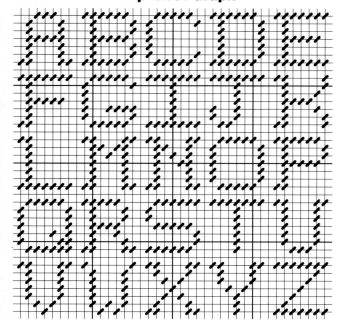

G – Pencil Box Side

(20w x 30h-hole pieces)
Cut 4 from 7-mesh & work.

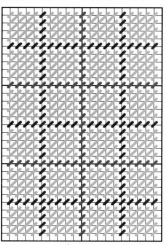

GILDED LACE ALBUM COVER

Lavish elegance on your treasured
photos with this fabulously feminine album cover.

SIZE

2" x 9¼" x 11¾" [5.1cm x 23.5cm x 29.8cm], not including lace, and covers a 1⅝" x 8¾" x 11¼" [4.1cm x 22.2cm x 28.6cm] photo album; photo window on frame is 3½" x 4⅝" [8.9cm x 11.7cm].

SKILL LEVEL: Average

MATERIALS
- 3½ sheets of 7-mesh plastic canvas
- 2¾ yds. [2.5m] white/gold metallic 2" [5.1cm] pregathered lace
- 36 white 3mm pearl beads
- Craft glue or glue gun
- Metallic cord; for amount see Color Key.
- Worsted-weight or plastic canvas yarn; for amount see Color Key.

CUTTING INSTRUCTIONS

A: For Frame, cut one according to graph.
B: For Cover Front and Back, cut two (one for Front and one for Back) 61w x 77h-holes (no graphs).
C: For Cover Spine, cut one 13w x 77h-holes (no graph).
D: For Cover Inside Flaps, cut two 20w x 77h-holes (no graphs).

STITCHING INSTRUCTIONS

NOTE: D pieces are not worked.

1: Using white and smyrna cross stitch, work A according to graph; work B and C pieces using established stitch pattern on A. With cord, overcast edges of A.

2: With cord, whipstitch B-D pieces together according to Cover Assembly Diagram.

3: Glue beads to right side of A as indicated on graph; glue lace around edges on wrong side of Frame (see photo), trimming away excess as needed. Leaving top edge unjoined for photo slot, glue Frame to center front of Cover (see photo).

4: Glue remaining lace around edges on inside of Cover (see photo), trimming away excess as needed to fit.

—Designed by Kimberly A. Suber

COLOR KEY: Gilded Lace Album Cover

Metallic cord		AMOUNT
☐	White/Gold	10 yds. [9.1m]

Worsted-weight		YARN AMOUNT
■	White	2 oz. [56.7g]

PLACEMENT KEY:
◙ Bead

A – Frame
(41w x 49h-hole piece) Cut 1 & work.

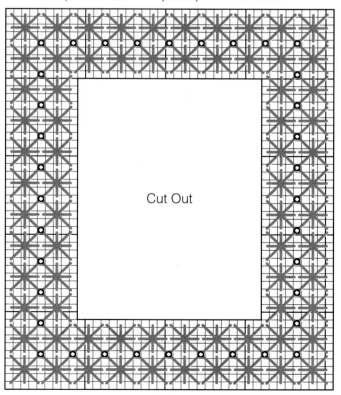

Cut Out

Cover Assembly Diagram
(inside view)

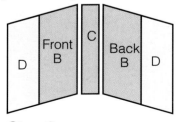

Step 1:
Holding B pieces wrong sides together with C between, whipstitch together.

Step 2:
Holding D pieces to wrong side of B pieces at outer edges, whipstitch outer edges together; overcast unfinished edges of B & C pieces.

LINKED-HEARTS BOUTIQUE SET

Lend love and lacy refinement to
your bedroom or bath with this graceful trio.

SIZES

Canister is 4" across x 5" tall [10.2cm x 12.7cm];
Frame is 6⅞" x 8¾" [17.5cm x 22.2cm] and has
a 2½" x 4¼" [6.4cm x 10.8cm] photo window;
Mirror Motif is 4⅜ x 4⅜ [11.1cm x 11.1cm].

SKILL LEVEL: Average

MATERIALS

- Two sheets of 7-mesh plastic canvas
- Two 6" [15.2cm] plastic canvas radial circles
- One white handheld mirror with 5¼"-across
  [13.3cm] round mirror back
- Craft glue or glue gun
- Worsted-weight or plastic canvas yarn; for
  amounts see Color Key.

CUTTING INSTRUCTIONS

A: For Canister Side, cut one 77w x 22h-holes (no graph).

B: For Canister Bottom, cut away outer eight rows of holes from one circle (no graph).

C: For Canister Lid, cut one from remaining circle according to graph.

D: For Canister Trim, cut one according to graph.

E: For Canister Handle, cut one 2w x 25h-holes (no graph).

F: For Frame Front, cut one according to graph.

G: For Frame Mat, cut one according to graph.

H: For Mirror Motif, cut one according to graph.

STITCHING INSTRUCTIONS

NOTE: B piece is not worked.

1: Using colors and stitches indicated, work A (Overlap five holes at ends as indicated on graph and work through both thicknesses at overlap area to join.), C, D and F-H pieces according to graphs; with white for Frame Front and sea green for Frame Mat, overcast cutout edges of F and G pieces. Overlapping two holes at end and working through both thicknesses at overlap area to join, using white and continental stitch, work E piece, overcast edges of E.

2: Using colors and embroidery stitches indicated, embroider detail on D and F-H pieces as indicated on graphs.

3: With sea green, whipstitch A and B pieces together, forming Canister; with white, whipstitch C and D pieces together, forming Canister Lid. With sea green, overcast Canister; Canister Lid is not overcast.

NOTE: Cut one 12½" [31.8cm], one 7" [17.8cm] and one 5½" [14cm] lengths of sea green.

4: For Canister Lid and Handle, glue 12½" strand around outside edge of trim; wrap 7" strand twice around Handle and glue to secure. Glue 5½" strand to Lid between rows of stitches (see photo). Glue seam of handle to center of Lid as shown.

5: For Frame, glue right side of G centered to wrong side of F; glue photo to back of G. Glue Mirror Motif to back of handheld mirror.

—Designed by Sandra Miller Maxfield

F – Frame Front
(45w x 57h-hole piece) Cut 1 & work.

COLOR KEY:
Linked-Hearts Boutique Set

Worsted-weight		YARN AMOUNT
	Sea Green	30 yds. [27.4m]
	Pink	25 yds. [22.9m]
	White	18 yds. [16.5m]
	Sail Blue	12 yds. [11m]
	Watermelon	11 yds. [10.1m]

STITCH KEY:
- – Backstitch/Straight
- • French Knot

H – Mirror Motif
(27w x 27h-hole piece) Cut 1 & work.

COLOR KEY: Linked-Hearts Boutique Set

Worsted-weight		YARN AMOUNT
▨	Sea Green	30 yds. [27.4m]
▨	Pink	25 yds. [22.9m]
▨	White	18 yds. [16.5m]
▨	Sail Blue	12 yds. [11m]
■	Watermelon	11 yds. [10.1m]

STITCH KEY:

⊟ Backstitch/Straight
⊡ French Knot

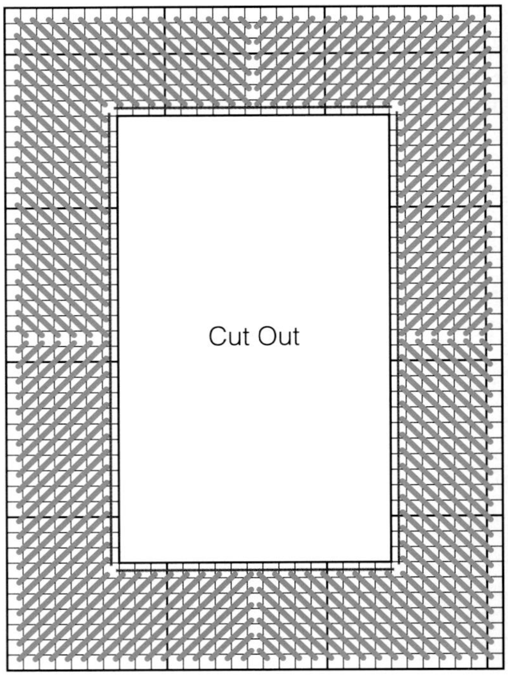

Canister Side Stitch Pattern Guide

Lap Over

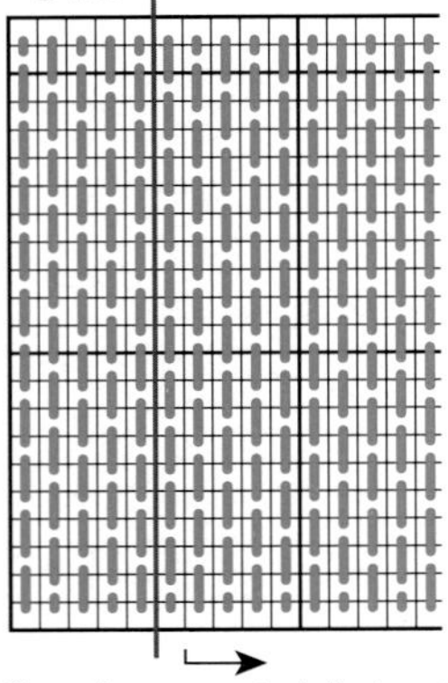

Continue established pattern across entire piece.

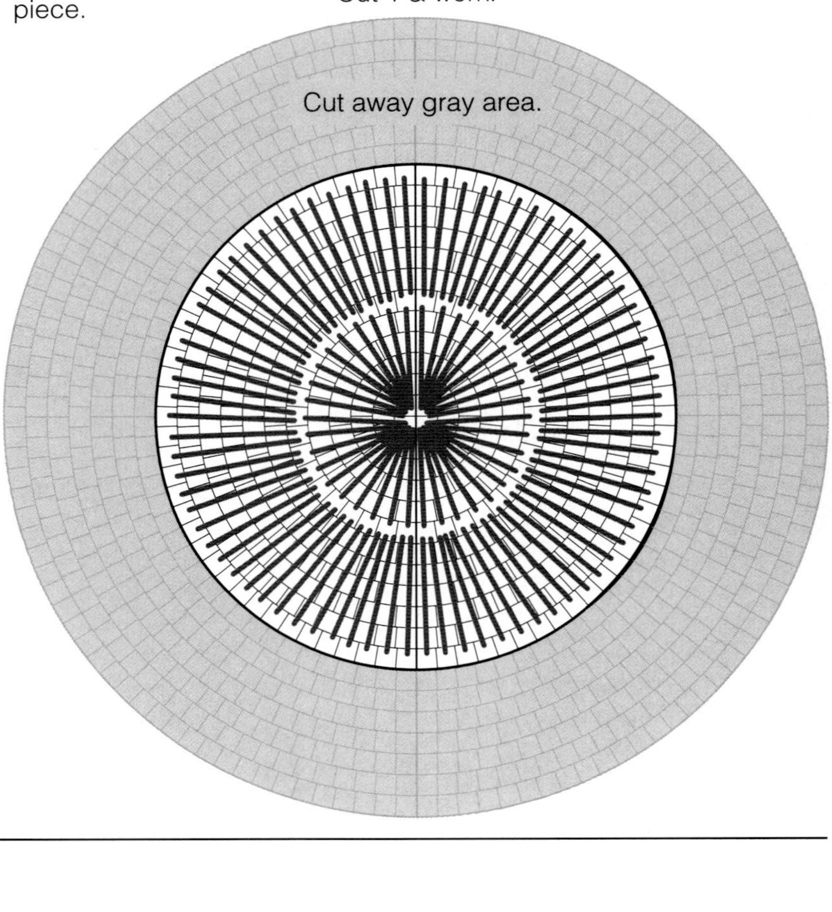

D – Canister Trim

(79w x 10h-hole piece) Cut 1 & work, overlapping holes & working through both thicknesses at overlap area to join.

Lap Over

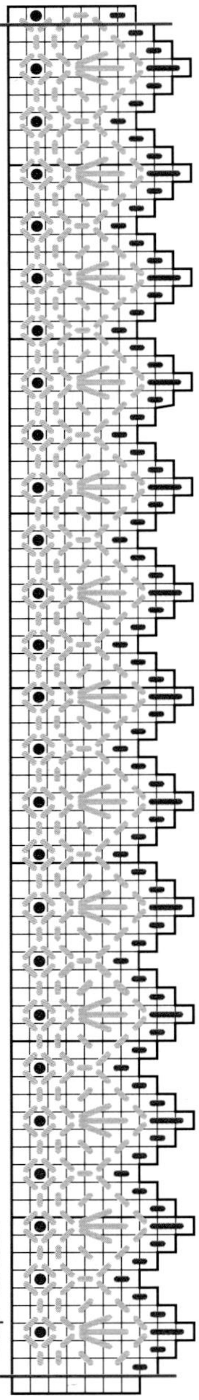

Lap Under

G – Frame Mat

(31w x 43h-hole piece) Cut 1 & work.

Cut Out

C – Canister Lid

(one 6" circle) Cut 1 & work.

Cut away gray area.

ANNOUNCEMENT FRAMES

*Rejoice over the birth of a special baby with
these frames that are perfect for proud parents to display or give as gifts.*

SIZE
Each is 6¼" x 8⅞" [15.9cm x 22.5cm], and has a
2⅞" x 3¾" [7.3cm x 9.5cm] photo window.

SKILL LEVEL: Average

MATERIALS
- 1½ sheets of 7-mesh plastic canvas
- ½ sheet of 10-mesh plastic canvas
- Craft glue or glue gun
- ⅛" [3mm] satin ribbon; for amount see individual Color Keys on page 96.
- Worsted-weight or plastic canvas yarn; for amounts see individual Color Keys.

CUTTING INSTRUCTIONS

NOTE: Use 10-mesh for B and 7-mesh plastic canvas for remaining pieces.

A: For Frame Front and Back, cut one according to graph for Front and one 40w x 58h-holes for Back (no Back graph).

B: For Letters and Punctuation Marks, cut number needed to spell corresponding announcement according to graphs.

C: For Boy Bottle, cut one according to graph.

D: For Boy Rattle, cut one according to graph.

E: For Girl Pacifier, cut one according to graph.

F: For Girl Carriage pieces, cut number indicated according to graphs.

STITCHING INSTRUCTIONS

NOTE: One A for Back is not worked.

1: For Frame, using white and scotch stitch, work one A for Front according to graph; overcast cutout edges.

2: Holding Back A to wrong side of Front A, starting and ending on right side at ◆ holes for vertical Frame or ▲ holes for horizontal Frame and leaving 6" [15.2cm] tails, using ribbon color indicated and running stitch and working through both thicknesses as indicated on graph, work A according to graph; tie ends into a bow and trim. With white, whipstitch A pieces together as indicated; overcast unfinished edges.

NOTE: For boy letters, separate 2 yds. [1.8m] of sail blue into 2-ply or nylon plastic canvas yarn into 1-ply strands.

3: For Boy Frame, with 2-ply (or 1-ply) strand, overcast edges of B pieces. Using colors and stitches indicated, work C and D pieces according to graphs; with matching colors, overcast edges. Glue motifs to Frame as desired or as shown in photo.

NOTE: For girl letters, separate 2 yds. [1.8m] of pink into 2-ply or nylon plastic canvas yarn into 1-ply strands.

4: For Girl Frame, with 2-ply (or 1-ply) strand, overcast edge of B pieces. Using color and stitches indicated, work E and F pieces according to graphs; with pink for Handle and Wheels, white for Carriage Body and with matching colors, overcast edges. Glue motifs to Frame as desired or as shown.

—Designed by Kimberly A. Suber

COLOR KEY: Girl Frame

⅛" ribbon	AMOUNT
■ Pink	1 yd. [0.9m]

Worsted-weight	YARN AMOUNT
⊘ White	30 yds. [27.4m]
▨ Pink	6 yds. [5.5m]
▨ Lemon	3 yds. [2.7m]
▨ Peach	1 yd. [0.9m]

COLOR KEY: Boy Frame

⅛" ribbon	AMOUNT
■ Blue	1 yd. [0.9m]

Worsted-weight	YARN AMOUNT
⊘ White	30 yds. [27.4m]
▨ Sail Blue	6 yds. [5.5m]
▨ Lt. Green	4 yds. [3.7m]
▨ Peach	1 yd. [0.9m]

B – Letters & Punctuation Marks
(cut number needed from 10-mesh)
Cut out pink areas carefully.

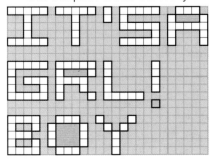

D – Boy Rattle
(9w x 21h-hole piece)
Cut 1 from 7-mesh & work

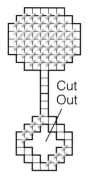

Cut
Out

E – Girl Pacifier
(10w x 17h-hole piece)
Cut 1 from 7-mesh & work.

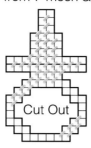

Cut Out

C – Boy Bottle
(8w x 21h-hole piece)
Cut 1 from 7-mesh & work.

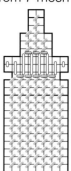

A – Frame Front
(40w x 58h-hole piece) Cut 1 from 7-mesh & work.
Whipstitch between green arrows.

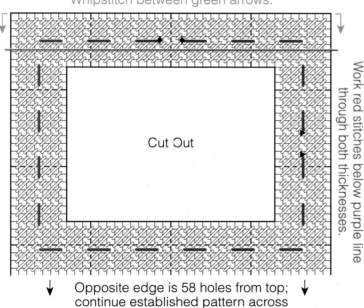

Cut Out

Work red stitches below purple line through both thicknesses.

Opposite edge is 58 holes from top;
continue established pattern across
entire length of piece.

F – Girl Carriage Body
(15w x 15h-hole piece)
Cut 1 from 7-mesh & work.

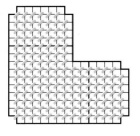

F – Girl Carriage Handle
(21w x 1h-hole piece)
Cut 1 from 7-mesh & work.

F – Girl Carriage Wheel
(8w x 8h-hole pieces)
Cut 2 from 7-mesh & work.

QUILTED HOUSE TRIO

These pretty quilted-look pieces are sure to perk up your kitchen or parlor.

SIZES

Place Mat is 12" x 15⅝" [30.5cm x 39.7cm]; Tissue Cover snugly covers a boutique-style tissue box; each Coaster is 3⅞" [9.8cm] square.

SKILL LEVEL: Easy

MATERIALS

- One 12" x 18" [30.5cm x 45.7cm] or larger and 2½ sheets of standard-size 7-mesh plastic canvas
- Worsted-weight or plastic canvas yarn; for amounts see Color Key.

CUTTING INSTRUCTIONS

NOTE: Use large sheet for Place Mat and standard-size canvas for remaining pieces.

A: For Place Mat, cut one from large sheet 103w x 79h-holes.

B: For Tissue Cover Top, cut one according to graph.

C: For Tissue Cover Sides, cut four 30w x 36h-holes.

D: For Coasters, cut four 25w x 25h-holes.

COLOR KEY: Quilted House Trio

Worsted-weight		YARN AMOUNT
	Pumpkin	3 oz. [85.1g]
	Royal	57 yds. [52.1m]
	Burgundy	54 yds. [49.4m]
	Gray	40 yds. [36.6m]
	Cinnamon	30 yds. [27.4m]
	Mermaid	23 yds. [21m]
	Forest	20 yds. [18.3m]
	Yellow	20 yds. [18.3m]

D – Coaster
(25w x 25h-hole pieces)
Cut 4 from standard-size sheet & work.

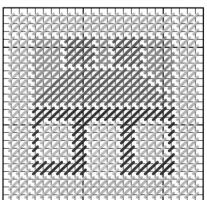

STITCHING INSTRUCTIONS

1: Using colors and stitches indicated, work pieces according to graphs. With burgundy, overcast edges of A and D pieces and cutout edges of B.

2: For Tissue Cover, with burgundy, whip-stitch B and C pieces together; overcast unfinished edges.

—*Designed by Michele Wilcox*

B – Tissue Cover Top
(30w x 30h-hole piece)
Cut 1 from standard-size sheet & work.

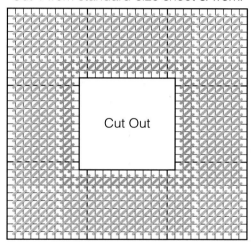

Cut Out

C – Tissue Cover Side
(30w x 36h-hole pieces) Cut 4 from standard-size sheet & work.

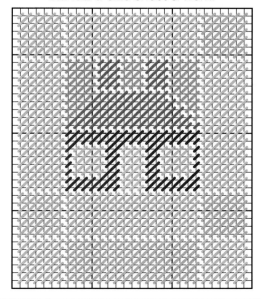

COLOR KEY: Quilted House Trio

Worsted-weight	YARN AMOUNT
Pumpkin	3 oz. [85.1g]
Royal	57 yds. [52.1m]
Burgundy	54 yds. [49.4m]
Gray	40 yds. [36.6m]
Cinnamon	30 yds. [27.4m]
Mermaid	23 yds. [21m]
Forest	20 yds. [18.3m]
Yellow	20 yds. [18.3m]

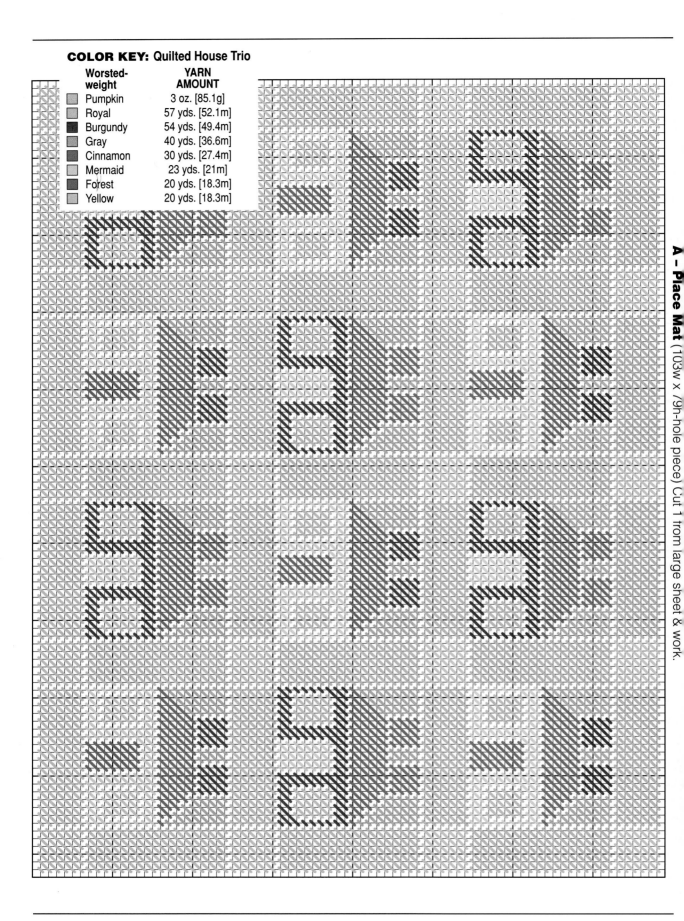

A – Place Mat (103w x 79h-hole piece) Cut 1 from large sheet & work.

SOUTHWEST FLAIR

Warm up your house or a friend's with these sweet-as-home accents.

SIZES

Plant Cozy is 6" across x 4⅞" tall [17.5cm x 12.4cm]; Tissue Cover loosely covers a boutique-style tissue box; Coaster is 3⅞" square [9.8cm]; Wall Plaque is 5¾" x 12¾" [14.6cm x 32.4cm], not including lace or hanger.

SKILL LEVEL: Easy

MATERIALS

- One 13½" x 22½" [34.3cm x 57.2cm] and one standard-size sheet of 7-mesh plastic canvas
- One 6" [15.2cm] plastic canvas radial circle
- 1 yd. [0.9m] white 1¼" [3.2cm] eyelet lace
- ½ yd. [0.5m] aqua ⅜" [10mm] satin ribbon
- One Velcro® closure (optional)
- Craft glue or glue gun
- Worsted-weight or plastic canvas yarn; for amounts see Color Key.

CUTTING INSTRUCTIONS

A: For Plant Cozy Side, cut one from large sheet 125w x 31h-holes.

B: For Plant Cozy Bottom, use 6" radial circle (no graph).

C: For Tissue Cover Top, cut one according to graph.

D: For Tissue Cover Sides, cut four 31w x 37h-holes.

E: For optional Tissue Cover Bottom and Flap, cut one 31w x 31h-holes for Bottom and one 31w x 12h-holes for Flap (no graphs).

F: For Coaster Front and Backing, cut two (one for Front and one for Backing) 25w x 25h-holes.

G: For Wall Plaque Front and Backing, cut two (one for Front and one for Backing) 84w x 37h-holes.

STITCHING INSTRUCTIONS

NOTE: B, E, one F for Backing and one G for Backing pieces are not worked.

1: Using colors and stitches indicated, work A, C, D, one F for Front and one G for front pieces according to graphs; fill in uncoded

C – Tissue Cover Top
(31w x 31h-hole piece) Cut 1 from standard-size sheet & work.

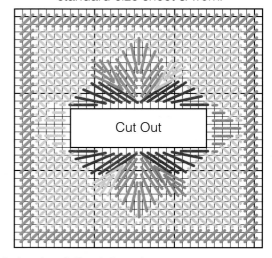

A – Plant Cozy Side (125w x 31h-hole piece) Cut 1 & work, overlapping ends & working through both thicknesses at overlap areas to join.

Lap Under

Lap Over

Continue established pattern across entire piece.

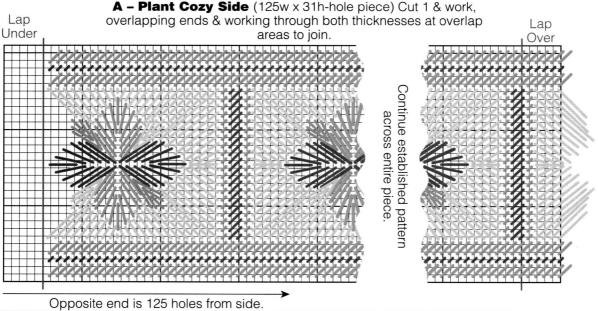

Opposite end is 125 holes from side.

areas of G using white and continental stitch. With burgundy, overcast cutout edges of C.

2: For Plant Cozy, with turquoise, whipstitch A and B pieces together; overcast unfinished edges.

3: For Tissue Cover, with turquoise, whipstitch C and D pieces together. For optional Tissue Cover Bottom, with turquoise, whipstitch E pieces together and to one D according to Tissue Cover Bottom Assembly Illustration. Overcast unfinished edges of Cover; glue closure to Flap and inside of Cover (see illustration).

4: For Coaster, holding Backing F to wrong side of Front F, with turquoise, whipstitch together.

5: For Wall Plaque, holding Backing G to wrong side of Front G, with turquoise, whipstitch together. Glue lace to wrong side around edges; for hanger, glue ends of ribbon to wrong side of Plaque (see photo).

—Designed by Debby Keel

D – Tissue Cover Side
(31w x 37h-hole pieces) Cut 4 from standard-size sheet & work.

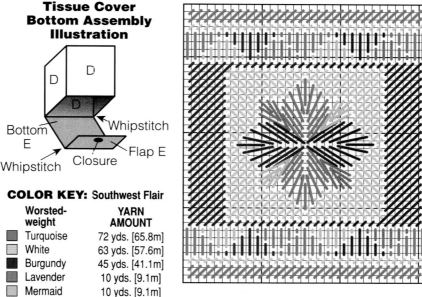

F – Coaster Front & Backing
(25w x 25h-hole pieces) Cut 2 from standard-size sheet. Work 1 for Front & leave 1 unworked for Backing.

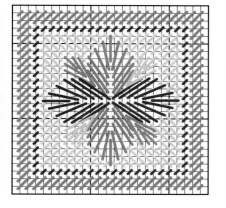

Tissue Cover Bottom Assembly Illustration

COLOR KEY: Southwest Flair

Worsted-weight		YARN AMOUNT
■	Turquoise	72 yds. [65.8m]
□	White	63 yds. [57.6m]
■	Burgundy	45 yds. [41.1m]
■	Lavender	10 yds. [9.1m]
▨	Mermaid	10 yds. [9.1m]

G – Wall Plaque Front & Backing
(84w x 37h-hole pieces) Cut 2 from standard-size sheets. Work 1 for Front & leave 1 unworked for Backing.

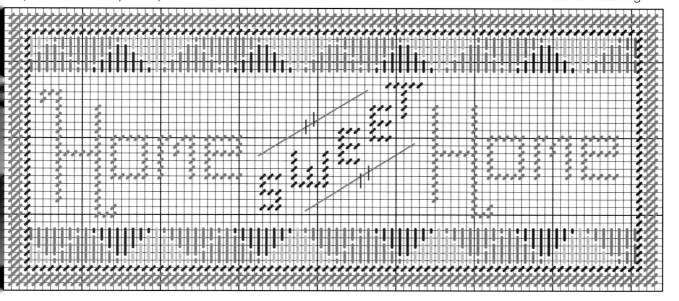

FAST FAMILY FAVORITES

TRIPLE CROSS TOTE

Take your favorite items along wherever you go in this handsome tote.

SIZE

2¾" x 10¼" square [7cm x 26cm], not including handles.

SKILL LEVEL: Average

MATERIALS

- 4½ sheets of ivory 7-mesh plastic canvas
- Worsted-weight or plastic canvas yarn; for amounts see Color Key.

CUTTING INSTRUCTIONS

A: For Front and Front Lining, cut two (one for Front and one for Front Lining) 67w x 67h-holes (no Front Lining graph).

B: For Back and Back Lining, cut two (one for Back and one for Back Lining) 67w x 67h-holes (no graphs).

C: For Sides and Side Linings, cut eight (four for Sides and four for Side Linings) 8w x 67h-holes (no Lining graph).

D: For Handles, cut two 6w x 70h-holes.

E: For Bottom, cut one 67w x 17h-holes (no graph).

STITCHING INSTRUCTIONS

NOTE: One A for Lining, B and four C pieces for Linings are not worked.

1: Using colors and stitches indicated, work one A for Front, four C for Sides and D pieces according to graphs, filling in each square on

COLOR KEY: Triple Cross Tote

Worsted-weight		YARN AMOUNT
▨	Eggshell	60 yds. [54.9m]
▧	Purple	25 yds. [22.9m]
☐	Lavender	18 yds. [16.5m]

OTHER:
☐ Triple Cross Stitch
☐ Handle Attachment

Tote Assembly Illustration
(Gray denotes wrong side.)

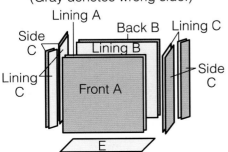

front using lavender and purple and Triple Cross Stitch (see illustration on page 106). With eggshell, overcast long edges of D pieces.

2: Holding Linings to wrong side of corresponding worked pieces, with eggshell, whipstitch together through all thicknesses according to Tote Assembly Illustration. Whipstitch unfinished top edges together, catching ends of Handles to join as indicated on graph.

—Designed by Carolyn Christmas

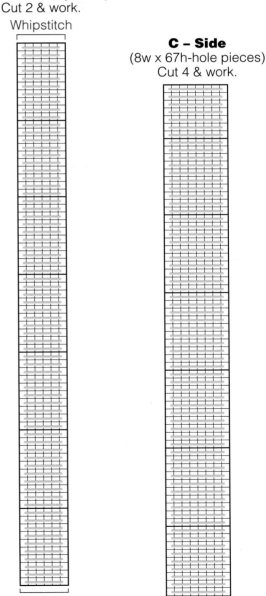

D – Handle
(6w x 70h-hole pieces)
Cut 2 & work.

Whipstitch

C – Side
(8w x 67h-hole pieces)
Cut 4 & work.

Whipstitch

Triple Cross Stitch Illustration

Step 1   **Step 2**   **Step 3**

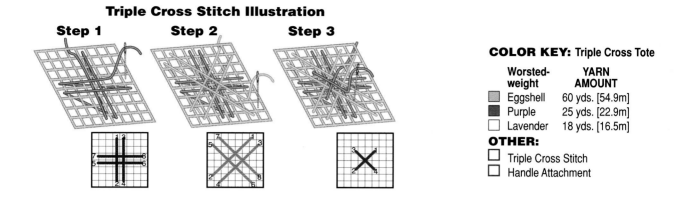

COLOR KEY: Triple Cross Tote

Worsted-weight	YARN AMOUNT
Eggshell	60 yds. [54.9m]
Purple	25 yds. [22.9m]
Lavender	18 yds. [16.5m]

OTHER:
☐ Triple Cross Stitch
☐ Handle Attachment

A – Front (67w x 67h-hole piece) Cut 1 & work.

Handle Attachment

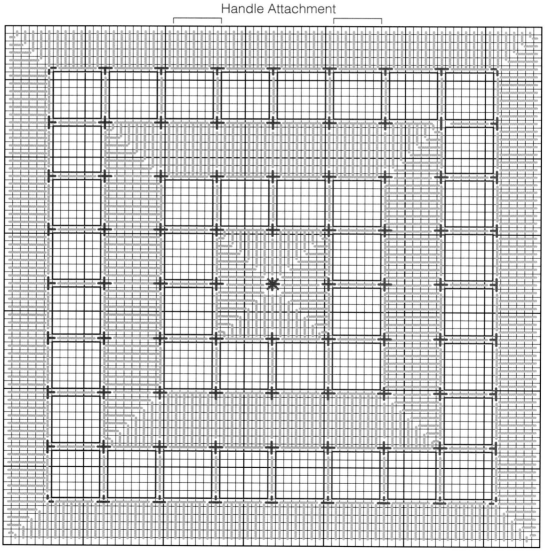

BLOOMING CONTAINERS

The bold and beautiful blooms of these
attractive accessories are sure to bring cheer to all who are near.

SIZES

Tissue Cover loosely covers a boutique-style tissue box; Trinket Box is 4¼" across x 4" tall [10.8cm x 10.2cm], not including flowers; each Coaster is 3¾" square [9.5cm]; Coaster Box is 1¾" x 4" x 4¾" [4.4cm x 10.2cm x 12.1cm], not including flowers.

SKILL LEVEL: Average

MATERIALS

• One sheet of 12" x 18" [30.5cm x 45.7cm] or larger and one standard-size sheet of 7-mesh plastic canvas
• One sheet of 10-mesh plastic canvas
• Two 4" [10.2cm] plastic canvas radial circles
• Thirteen white 13mm azalea flower beads
• Velcro® closure (optional)
• Craft glue or glue gun
• Six-strand embroidery floss; for amounts see Color Key.
• Worsted-weight or plastic canvas yarn; for amounts see Color Key.

CUTTING INSTRUCTIONS

NOTE: Use large sheet for D and G pieces, 7-mesh for A-N pieces and 10-mesh canvas for remaining pieces.

A: For Tissue Cover Sides, cut four 32w x 37h-holes.

B: For Tissue Cover Top, cut one according to graph.

C: For Tissue Cover optional Bottom and Flap, cut one 32w x 32h-holes for Bottom and one 32w x 12h-holes for Flap (no graphs).

D: For Trinket Box Side, cut one 92w x 25h-holes (no graph).

E: For Trinket Box Bottom, cut away one outer row of holes from one 4" circle (no graph).

F: For Trinket Box Lid, use remaining 4" circle (no graph).

G: For Trinket Box Lid Lip, cut one according to graph.

H: For Coasters, cut six 24w x 24h-holes.

I: For Coaster Box Sides, cut two according to graph.

J: For Coaster Box Ends, cut two according to graph.

K: For Coaster Box Bottom, cut one 28w x 8h-holes (no graph).

L: For Coaster Box Lid Sides, cut two according to graph.

M: For Coaster Box Lid Ends, cut two according to graph.

N: For Coaster Box Lid Top, cut one 30w x 10h-holes (no graph).

M – Coaster Box Lid End
(10w x 13h-hole pieces)
Cut 2 from 7-mesh & work.

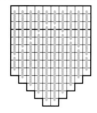

Q – Single Leaf
(14w x 9h-hole pieces)
Cut 4 from
10-mesh & work.

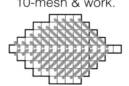

H – Coaster
(24w x 24h-hole pieces)
Cut 6 from 7-mesh & work.

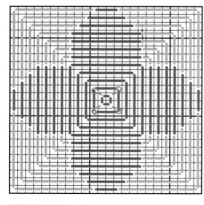

I – Coaster Box Side
(28w x 19h-hole pieces)
Cut 2 from 7-mesh & work.

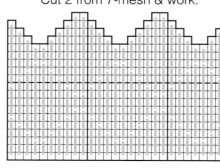

COLOR KEY: Blooming Containers

Embroidery floss	AMOUNT
■ Green	70 yds. [64m]
■ Dk. Blue	25 yds. [22.9m]
□ Purple	20 yds. [18.3m]
□ Red	20 yds. [18.3m]

Worsted-weight	YARN AMOUNT
■ Eggshell	2 oz. [56.7g]
■ Fern	32 yds. [29.3m]
■ Purple	6 yds. [5.5m]
□ Red	6 yds. [5.5m]
□ Royal Dark	6 yds. [5.5m]
■ White	3 yds. [2.7m]

STITCH KEY:
⬯ Lazy Daisy
✦ Flower Bead Attachment

O: For Petals, cut twenty-six according to graph.

P: For Leaf Clusters, cut ten according to graph.

Q: For Single Leaves, cut four according to graph.

STITCHING INSTRUCTIONS

NOTE: C and E pieces are not worked.

1: For Tissue Cover, using colors and stitches indicated, work A and B pieces according to graphs. With eggshell, overcast unfinished cutout edges of B; whipstitch A and B pieces together forming Cover. For optional Cover Bottom, whipstitch C pieces together and to Cover according to Optional Cover Bottom Assembly Illustration on page 110. Overcast unfinished edges of Cover; if desired, glue closure to Flap.

2: For Trinket Box, using eggshell and long stitch, work D (Overlap short edges six holes, work through both thicknesses at overlap area to join.) according to Trinket Box Side Stitch Pattern Guide. (*NOTE: Pattern will not end evenly.*) Whipstitch D and E pieces together.

3: Using eggshell and stitches indicated, work F according to Trinket Box Lid Top Stitch Pattern Guide. Overlapping ends as indicated and working as for Side, work G according to graph. Whipstitch F and G pieces together; overcast unfinished edges of Box and Lid.

4: For Coasters, using colors and stitches indicated, work two H pieces according to graph; substituting royal dark and red for purple, work two Coasters in each color according to graph. With fern, overcast unfinished edges. Using white and lazy daisy stitch, embroider flower centers as indicated.

5: For Coaster Box, using eggshell and stitches indicated, work I, J, L and M pieces according to graphs. Using eggshell and long stitch over narrow width, work K and N pieces. Whipstitch I-K pieces together, forming Box, whip-

stitch L and M pieces together, forming Lid; overcast unfinished edges.

6: Using six strands dark blue and stitches indicated, work ten O pieces according to graph; substituting red and purple for dark blue, work eight O pieces in each color according to graph. With matching colors, overcast unfinished edges. Using six strands green and stitches indicated, work P and Q pieces according to graphs; overcast unfinished edges.

7: For each flower, holding two matching color O pieces together (See Flower Assembly Illustration on page 110), with matching color, tack together at center. To attach flower bead, using matching color, work a French knot through O pieces and center of bead. Glue flowers and leaves to Cover and Boxes as shown in photo.

—*Designed by Patricia Hall*

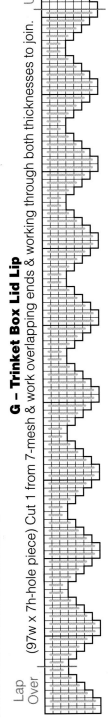

G – Trinket Box Lid Lip
(97w x 7h-hole piece) Cut 1 from 7-mesh & work overlapping ends & working through both thicknesses to join.

Lap Under

Lap Over

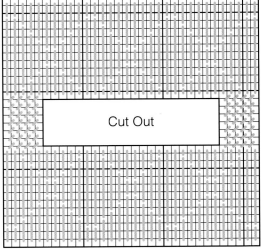

B – Tissue Cover Top
(32w x 32h-hole piece)
Cut 1 from 7-mesh & work.

Cut Out

COLOR KEY: Blooming Containers

Embroidery floss	AMOUNT
Green	70 yds. [64m]
Dk. Blue	25 yds. [22.9m]
Purple	20 yds. [18.3m]
Red	20 yds. [18.3m]

Worsted-weight	YARN AMOUNT
Eggshell	2 oz. [56.7g]
Fern	32 yds. [29.3m]
Purple	6 yds. [5.5m]
Red	6 yds. [5.5m]
Royal Dark	6 yds. [5.5m]
White	3 yds. [2.7m]

STITCH KEY:

⊖ Lazy Daisy
✦ Flower Bead Attachment

P – Leaf Cluster
(19w x 20h-hole pieces)
Cut 10 from 10-mesh & work.

L – Coaster Box Lid Side
(30w x 13h-hole pieces)
Cut 2 from 7-mesh & work.

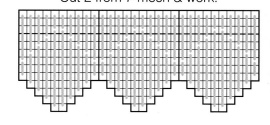

Coaster Box Assembly Illustration
(Pieces are shown in different colors for contrast; gray denotes wrong side.)

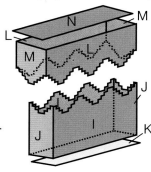

A – Tissue Cover Side
(32w x 37h-hole pieces) Cut 4 from 7-mesh & work.

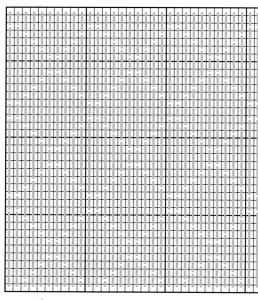

J – Coaster Box End
(8w x 18h-hole pieces)
Cut 2 from 7-mesh & work.

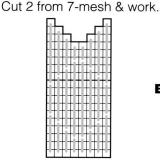

Optional Cover Bottom Assembly Illustration

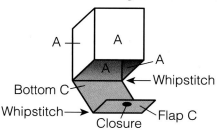

A — A
Bottom C — Whipstitch
Whipstitch — Closure — Flap C

Trinket Box Side Stitch Pattern Guide

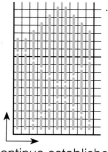

Continue established pattern up and across each entire piece.

Flower Assembly Illustration

Flower Bead

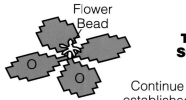

O – Petals
(7w x 17h-hole pieces)
Cut 26 from 10-mesh & work.

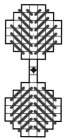

Trinket Box Lid Top Stitch Pattern Guide
Cut away gray area.

Continue established pattern around entire piece using a complete 4" circle.

QUICK HOLIDAY FUN

LILIES BIBLE COVER

Keep sacred sentiments near your heart with this beautiful lilies Bible cover.

SIZE

Covers a 2" x 7" x 9½" [5.1cm x 17.8cm x 24.1cm] Bible. To make a larger Cover, using book binding as a guide, cut pieces to fit. Center C over stitch pattern on center of Front A; fill in expanded border using sail blue and long stitch.

SKILL LEVEL: Average

MATERIALS

- 2¼ sheets of 7-mesh plastic canvas
- Six-strand embroidery floss; for amount see Color Key.
- Metallic cord; for amount see Color Key.
- Worsted-weight or plastic canvas yarn; for amounts see Color Key.

CUTTING INSTRUCTIONS

A: For Front and Back, cut two (one for

Front and one for Back) 52w x 71h-holes (no Back graph).

B: For Spine, cut one 14w x 71h-holes (no graph).

C: For Inside Flaps, cut two 17w x 71h-holes (no graph).

STITCHING INSTRUCTIONS

1: Using colors and stitches indicated, work one A for Front according to graph. Using sail blue and long stitch over five bars, work one A for Back, B and C pieces according to background pattern established on Front A.

2: Using six strands floss and embroidery stitches indicated, embroider stamens as indicated on graph.

3: With sail blue, whipstitch A-C pieces together according to Cover Assembly Diagram; overcast unfinished edges.

—Designed by Kathleen Hurley

COLOR KEY: Lilies Bible Cover

	Embroidery floss	**AMOUNT**
■	Black	2 yds. [1.8m]
	Metallic cord	**AMOUNT**
■	Gold	2 yds. [1.8m]
	Worsted-weight	**YARN AMOUNT**
□	Sail Blue	3 oz. [85.1g]
■	White	7 yds. [6.4m]
■	Silver	6 yds. [5.5m]
■	Fern	5 yds. [4.6m]
■	Moss	2 yds. [1.8m]
□	Lemon	1 yd. [0.9m]

STITCH KEY:

- ⊟ Backstitch/Straight
- ⊙ French Knot

Cover Assembly Diagram
(inside view)

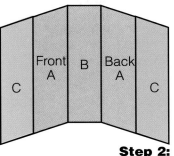

Step 1:
Holding A pieces wrong sides together with B between, whipstitch together.

Step 2:
Holding C pieces wrong sides together with Front & Back at matching outside edges, whipstitch together.

A – Front
(52w x 71h-hole piece) Cut 1 & work.

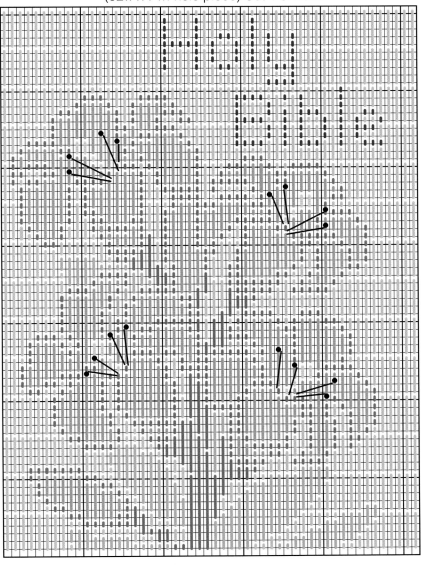

BUNNY CHALET

Keep a handle on your Easter festivities with this delightful
bunny house container for treats, flowers or anything else to bring joy to the holiday.

SIZE
6½" x 10¼" x 11" tall [16.5cm x 26cm x 27.9cm], including handle.

SKILL LEVEL: Average

MATERIALS
• 2½ sheets of 7-mesh plastic canvas
• Craft glue or glue gun
• Worsted-weight or plastic canvas yarn;
  for amounts see Color Key.

CUTTING INSTRUCTIONS
A: For Cottage Front and Back, cut two (one for Front and one for Back) according to graph.

B: For Cottage Sides, cut two 29w x 25h-holes.

C: For Cottage Bottom, cut one 57w x 29h-holes (no graph).

D: For Roof Side Pieces, cut two according to graph.

E: For Roof Top Pieces, cut two 27w x 7h-holes.

F: For Handle, cut one according to graph.

G: For Bunny, cut one according to graph.

H: For Windows, cut six according to graph.

I: For Door, cut one according to graph.

J: For Flowers, cut four according to graph.

K: For Eggs, cut four according to graph.

STITCHING INSTRUCTIONS
NOTE: C is not worked.

1: Using colors and stitches indicated, work A, B and D-K pieces according to graphs. With baby green for Eggs, white for Door, pink for

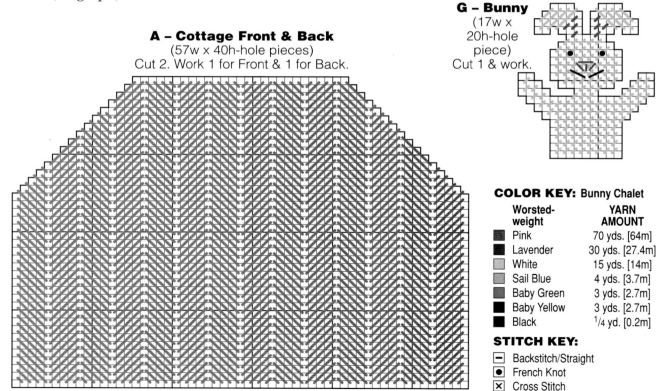

A – Cottage Front & Back
(57w x 40h-hole pieces)
Cut 2. Work 1 for Front & 1 for Back.

G – Bunny
(17w x 20h-hole piece)
Cut 1 & work.

COLOR KEY: Bunny Chalet

Worsted-weight	YARN AMOUNT
Pink	70 yds. [64m]
Lavender	30 yds. [27.4m]
White	15 yds. [14m]
Sail Blue	4 yds. [3.7m]
Baby Green	3 yds. [2.7m]
Baby Yellow	3 yds. [2.7m]
Black	¼ yd. [0.2m]

STITCH KEY:
▬	Backstitch/Straight
⊙	French Knot
☒	Cross Stitch

Handle and with matching colors, over-cast edges of F-K pieces.

2: Using colors (Separate into individual plies, if desired.) and embroidery stitches indicated, embroider detail on F, G, I and K pieces as indicated on graphs.

3: Whipstitch and assemble A-F pieces as indicated and according to Cottage Assembly Diagram on page 116.

4: Glue Door, Windows, Flowers and Eggs around Cottage as shown in photo; glue Bunny to inside of Front near Handle as shown.

—*Designed by Robin Petrina*

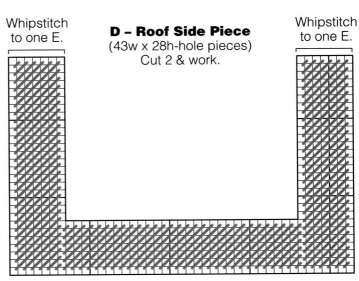

Whipstitch to one E.

D – Roof Side Piece
(43w x 28h-hole pieces)
Cut 2 & work.

Whipstitch to one E.

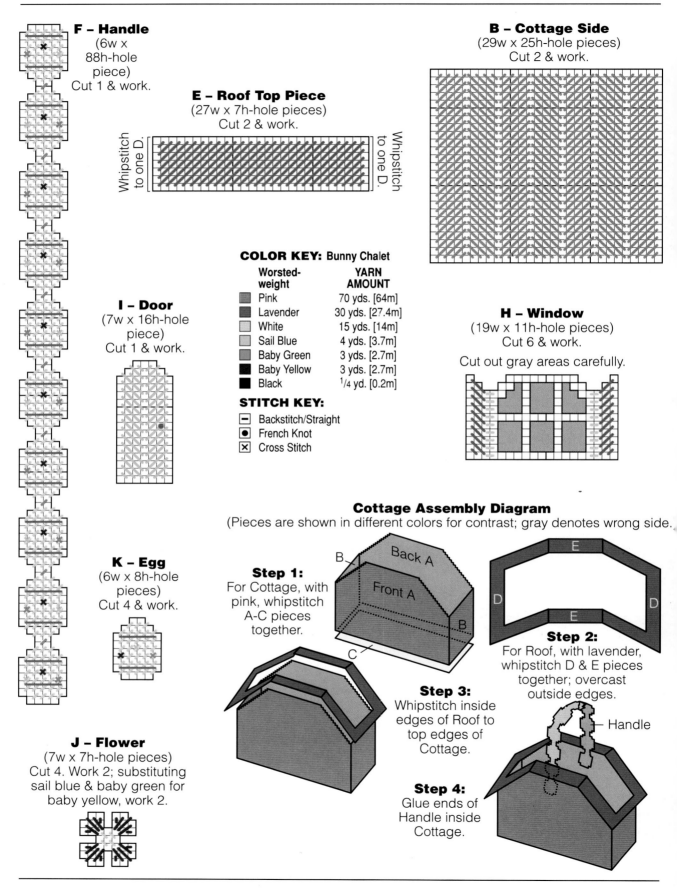

F – Handle
(6w x 88h-hole piece)
Cut 1 & work.

E – Roof Top Piece
(27w x 7h-hole pieces)
Cut 2 & work.

Whipstitch to one D.

Whipstitch to one D.

B – Cottage Side
(29w x 25h-hole pieces)
Cut 2 & work.

COLOR KEY: Bunny Chalet

Worsted-weight	YARN AMOUNT
Pink	70 yds. [64m]
Lavender	30 yds. [27.4m]
White	15 yds. [14m]
Sail Blue	4 yds. [3.7m]
Baby Green	3 yds. [2.7m]
Baby Yellow	3 yds. [2.7m]
Black	1/4 yd. [0.2m]

STITCH KEY:
- – Backstitch/Straight
- ● French Knot
- ☒ Cross Stitch

I – Door
(7w x 16h-hole piece)
Cut 1 & work.

H – Window
(19w x 11h-hole pieces)
Cut 6 & work.

Cut out gray areas carefully.

K – Egg
(6w x 8h-hole pieces)
Cut 4 & work.

Cottage Assembly Diagram
(Pieces are shown in different colors for contrast; gray denotes wrong side.)

Step 1:
For Cottage, with pink, whipstitch A-C pieces together.

Step 2:
For Roof, with lavender, whipstitch D & E pieces together; overcast outside edges.

Step 3:
Whipstitch inside edges of Roof to top edges of Cottage.

Step 4:
Glue ends of Handle inside Cottage.

Handle

B Back A

Front A

B

C

E

D

E

D

J – Flower
(7w x 7h-hole pieces)
Cut 4. Work 2; substituting sail blue & baby green for baby yellow, work 2.

PINWHEELS & PATTERNS

*Pretty and perky pinwheels are sure to
please all ages with their striking colors and fun design!*

SIZES

Pinwheel Place Mat is 10⅜" x 13½" [26.3cm x
34.3cm]; Pinwheel Coaster is 3⅞" square
[9.8cm]; Pinwheel Napkin Ring is 2" across
[5.1cm]; Pattern Place Mat is 10½" x 13½"
[26.7cm x 34.3cm]; Pattern Coaster is 3¾"
square [9.5cm]; Pattern Napkin Ring is 1⅞"
across [4.8cm].

SKILL LEVEL: Average

MATERIALS FOR ALL

- 1⅓ sheets of dk. blue, one sheet of red and ½
  sheet of clear 7-mesh plastic canvas
- 3⅝"-square [9.2cm] piece of 14-count metallic
  gold perforated paper
- Craft glue or glue gun
- Metallic cord; for amount see Color Key
  on page 118.
- Worsted-weight or plastic canvas yarn; for
  amounts see Color Key.

PINWHEEL
CUTTING INSTRUCTIONS
A: For Place Mat, cut one from dk. blue 90w x 69h-holes (no graph).

B: For Coaster Front and Backing, cut two from dk. blue (one for Front and one for Backing) 25w x 25h-holes (no Backing graph).

C: For Napkin Ring Band, cut one from clear 37w x 2h-holes.

D: For Napkin Ring Motif, cut one from clear according to graph.

STITCHING INSTRUCTIONS
NOTE: One B for Backing is not worked.

1: Using colors and stitches indicated (See Running Stitch Illustration.) and omitting stitches around outer edges of B (see photo), work A (*NOTE: Center area of A is not worked; see photo.*), one B for Front, C and D pieces according to graphs and stitch pattern guide.

2: Holding Backing to wrong side of Front, using gold cord and running stitch over one bar, work stitches around outer edges of B pieces through both thicknesses as one according to graph.

3: With royal, overcast edges of C and D pieces; glue D to C over seam edges, forming Napkin Ring.

PATTERNS
CUTTING INSTRUCTIONS
A: For Place Mat, use red 70w x 90h-hole sheet (no graph).

B: For Coaster, cut one from clear 24w x 24h-holes.

C: For Napkin Ring, cut one from clear 42w x 12h-holes.

STITCHING INSTRUCTIONS
1: Using colors and stitches indicated and omitting center area of A (see photo), work pieces according to graphs and stitch pattern guide.

2: With royal, overcast edges. Glue perforated paper to back of B for lining.

—Designed by Mary T. Cosgrove

COLOR KEY: Pinwheels & Patterns

	Metallic cord	AMOUNT
▨	Gold	9 yds. [8.2m]

	Worsted-weight	YARN AMOUNT
■	Royal	25 yds. [22.9m]
■	Red	9 yds. [8.2m]
▨	White	9 yds. [8.2m]

C – Pinwheel Napkin Ring Band
(37w x 2h-hole piece)
Cut 1 from clear & work, overlapping ends as indicated & working through both thicknesses at overlap area to join.

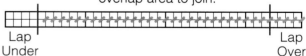

Lap Under   Lap Over

D – Pinwheel Napkin Ring Motif
(12w x 12h-hole piece)
Cut 1 from clear & work.

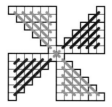

C – Pattern Napkin Ring
(42w x 12h-hole piece)
Cut 1 from clear & work, overlapping ends as indicated & working through both thicknesses at overlap area to join.

Lap Over   Lap Under

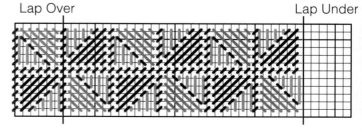

B – Patterns Coaster
(24w x 24h-hole piece)
Cut 1 from clear & work.

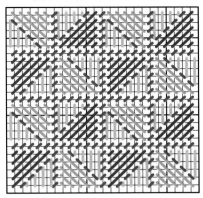

B – Pinwheel Coaster
(25w x 25h-hole piece)
Cut 1 from dk. blue & work.

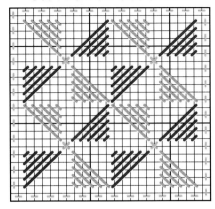

Patterns Place Mat
Stitch Pattern Guide

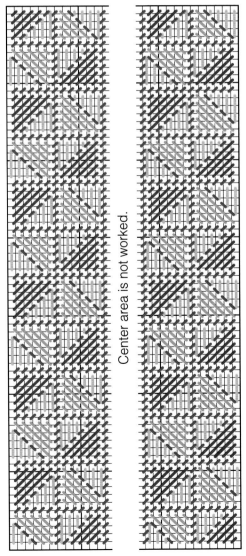

Center area is not worked.

Pinwheel Place Mat
Stitch Pattern Guide

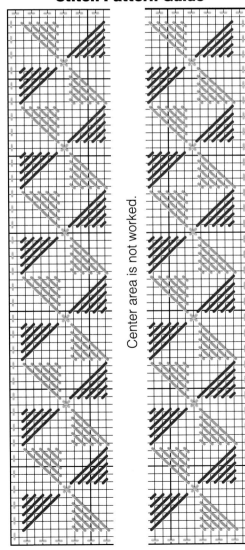

Center area is not worked.

BIRDHOUSE DOORSTOP

*Uncle Sam's favorite colors and
patterns make this a truly patriotic birdhouse doorstop.*

SIZE
3⅜" x 5¼" x 9¾" tall [8.6cm x 13.3cm x 24.8cm].

SKILL LEVEL: Average

MATERIALS
- 1½ sheets of 7-mesh plastic canvas
- 2" x 5" x 7½" [5.1cm x 12.7cm x 19cm] brick or other weighting material
- Craft glue or glue gun
- Worsted-weight or plastic canvas yarn; for amounts see Color Key.

CUTTING INSTRUCTIONS
   A: For Front, cut one according to graph.
   B: For Back, cut one according to graph.
   C: For Sides, cut two 16w x 51h-holes.
   D: For Roof Sides, cut two 22w x 24h-holes.
   E: For Optional Bottom, cut one 26w x 16h-holes (no graph).

STITCHING INSTRUCTIONS
NOTE: E is not worked.

1: Using colors and stitches indicated, work A-D pieces according to graphs. With royal, whipstitch A-C pieces together according to Doorstop Assembly Illustration; if desired, whipstitch E to bottom. Overcast unfinished edges.

2: Holding D pieces wrong sides together, with royal, whipstitch together as indicated on graph; overcast unfinished edges.

3: Place weight inside Doorstop; glue roof to Doorstop. Display as desired.
                          —*Designed by Michele Wilcox*

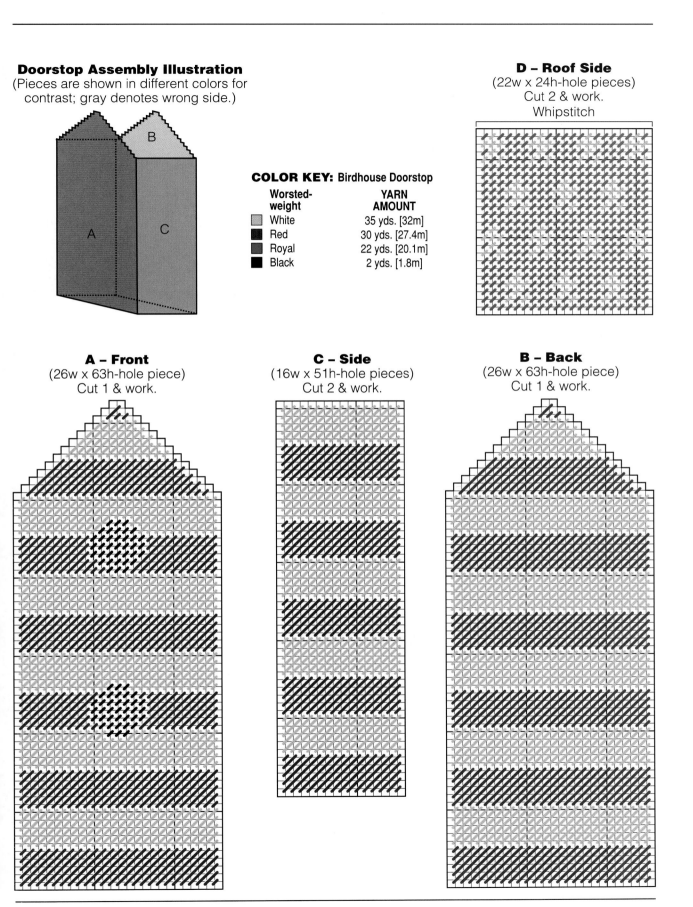

Doorstop Assembly Illustration
(Pieces are shown in different colors for contrast; gray denotes wrong side.)

COLOR KEY: Birdhouse Doorstop

Worsted-weight	YARN AMOUNT
White	35 yds. [32m]
Red	30 yds. [27.4m]
Royal	22 yds. [20.1m]
Black	2 yds. [1.8m]

D – Roof Side
(22w x 24h-hole pieces)
Cut 2 & work.
Whipstitch

A – Front
(26w x 63h-hole piece)
Cut 1 & work.

C – Side
(16w x 51h-hole pieces)
Cut 2 & work.

B – Back
(26w x 63h-hole piece)
Cut 1 & work.

SUMMER SPECTACULAR

Have a spectacular summer splash with
these coasters with holder, welcome sign and flag box.

PINEAPPLE WELCOME

SIZE
7⅜" x 10½" [18.7cm x 26.7cm].

SKILL LEVEL: Easy

MATERIALS
- One sheet of 7-mesh plastic canvas
- Worsted-weight or plastic canvas yarn; for amounts see Color Key.

CUTTING INSTRUCTIONS
For Pineapple Welcome, cut one according to graph.

STITCHING INSTRUCTIONS
1: Using colors and stitches indicated, work piece according to graph. With forest for leaves and with matching colors as shown in photo, overcast edges.

2: Hang or display as desired.

—Designed by Michele Wilcox

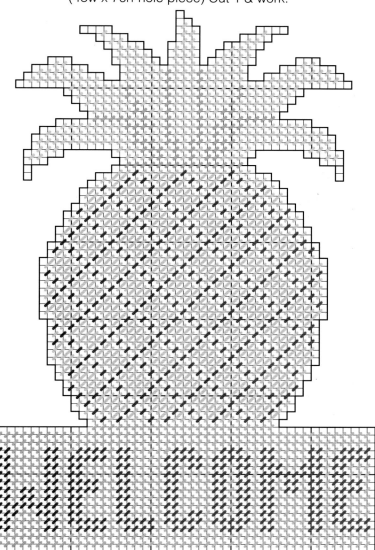

Pineapple Welcome
(48w x 70h-hole piece) Cut 1 & work.

COLOR KEY: Pineapple Welcome

Worsted-weight	YARN AMOUNT
Yellow	20 yds. [18.3m]
Fern	13 yds. [11.9m]
Eggshell	10 yds. [9.1m]
Maple	8 yds. [7.3m]
Royal	6 yds. [5.5m]
Burgundy	4 yds. [3.7m]
Forest	3 yds. [2.7m]

STARS & STRIPES

SIZE
4¼" x 5¾" x 3¾" tall [10.8cm x 14.6cm x 9.5cm].

SKILL LEVEL: Average

MATERIALS
- Three sheets of 7-mesh plastic canvas
- One 3" [7.6cm] piece of cardboard
- Worsted-weight or plastic canvas yarn; for amounts see Color Key on page 124.

CUTTING INSTRUCTIONS

A: For Box Sides, cut two 35w x 22h-holes (no graph).

B: For Box Ends, cut two 25w x 22h-holes (no graph).

C: For Box Bottom, cut one 35w x 25h-holes (no graph).

D: For Lid Top, cut one 37w x 27h-holes.

E: For Lid Sides, cut two 37w x 7h-holes (no graph).

F: For Lid Ends, cut two 27w x 7h-holes (no graph).

STITCHING INSTRUCTIONS

1: Using colors and stitches indicated, work pieces according to graphs and stitch pattern guides.

2: Using eggshell and French knot, embroider stars on D as indicated on graph.

3: Whipstitch pieces together according to Box & Lid Assembly Diagram; with red, overcast unfinished edges.

NOTE: Cut eight 4" [10.2cm] lengths of gold.

4: For each tassel (make 4), wrap gold yarn around cardboard ten times. Slide loops off cardboard and tie one 4" strand around all loops ½" [13mm] from fold. Cut through loops. Thread each end of hanger strand from front to back through ▲ holes on corners of D as indicated; knot ends at back to secure and trim ends close to knot.

—Designed by Michele Wilcox

Box End & Bottom Stitch Pattern Guide

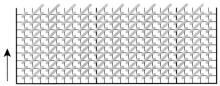

Continue established pattern across each entire piece.

D – Lid Top (37w x 27h-hole piece) Cut 1 & work.

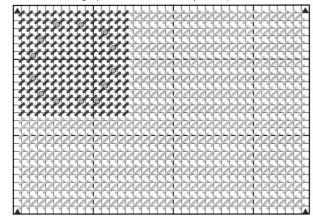

Lid Side Stitch Pattern Guide

Continue established pattern across each entire piece.

Box Side & Lid End Stitch Pattern Guide

Continue established pattern up & across each entire piece.

COLOR KEY: Stars & Stripes

Worsted-weight	YARN AMOUNT
☐ Eggshell	32 yds. [29.3m]
☐ Red	30 yds. [27.4m]
☐ Gold	10 yds. [9.1m]
☐ Royal	3 yds. [2.7m]

STITCH KEY:
- ⊙ French Knot
- ▲ Tassel Attachment

Box & Lid Assembly Diagram

Step 1:
With red, whipstitch A-C pieces together, forming box.

Step 2:
(underside view)
With gold for top edges & with red, whipstitch D-F pieces together; forming lid.

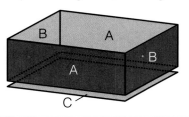

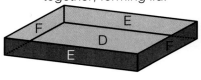

QUILT SQUARES

SIZES
Holder is 2⅝" x 4" x 4¾" tall [6.7cm x 10.2cm x 12.1cm]; each Coaster is 3¾"-square [8.2cm].

SKILL LEVEL: Average

MATERIALS
- Two sheets of 7-mesh plastic canvas
- Craft glue or glue gun
- Worsted-weight or plastic canvas yarn; for amounts see Color Key.

CUTTING INSTRUCTIONS
A: For Holder Sides and Bottom, cut three (two for Sides and one for Bottom) 26w x 16h-holes (no graphs).

B: For Holder Ends, cut two 16w x 16h-holes (no graph).

C: For Holder Handles, cut two 3w x 38h-holes (no graphs).

D: For Coasters #1-#4, cut one each 24w x 24h-holes.

STITCHING INSTRUCTIONS
1: Using eggshell and stitches indicated, work A, B and D pieces according to graphs and Holder Stitch Pattern Guide. Using eggshell and continental stitch, work C pieces; with burgundy for Handles and eggshell for Coasters, overcast edges of C and D pieces.

2: With burgundy, whipstitch A and B pieces together according to Holder Assembly Illustration; overcast unfinished edges. Glue Handles inside Holder according to illustration.

—Designed by Michele Wilcox

COLOR KEY: Quilt Squares

Worsted-weight	YARN AMOUNT
Eggshell	35 yds. [32m]
Burgundy	6 yds. [5.5m]
Lavender	6 yds. [5.5m]
Mermaid	6 yds. [5.5m]
Sail Blue	6 yds. [5.5m]

Holder Stitch Pattern Guide

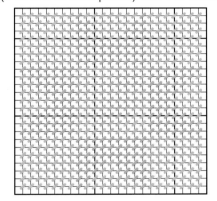

Continue established pattern up & across each entire piece.

Holder Assembly Illustration
(Gray denotes wrong side.)

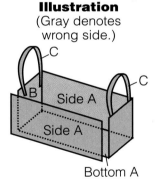

D – Coaster #1
(24w x 24h-hole piece) Cut 1 & work.

D – Coaster #2
(24w x 24h-hole piece) Cut 1 & work.

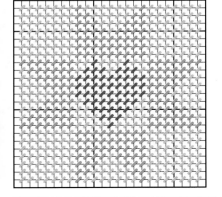

D – Coaster #3
(24w x 24h-hole piece) Cut 1 & work.

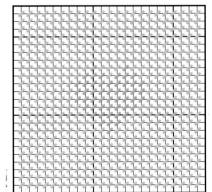

D – Coaster #4
(24w x 24h-hole piece) Cut 1 & work.

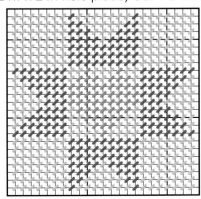

Sign (70w x 90h-hole piece) Cut 1 & work.

Trick-or-Treat Party

Treat all your little tricksters to this spooky Halloween greeting.

SIZE
10⅝" x 13⅝" [27cm x 34.6cm].

SKILL LEVEL: Easy

MATERIALS
- One sheet of 7-mesh plastic canvas
- Metallic cord; for amount see Color Key.
- Worsted-weight or plastic canvas yarn; for amounts see Color Key.

CUTTING INSTRUCTIONS
For Sign, cut one according to graph.

STITCHING INSTRUCTIONS
1: Using colors and stitches indicated, work piece according to graph. With cord, overcast edges.

2: Using yarn in colors indicated and straight stitch, embroider detail as indicated on graph.

NOTE: *Cut one 12" [30.5cm] length of bt. orange.*

3: Tie strand into a bow and glue to Sign as shown in photo. Hang as desired.

—*Designed by Mary T. Cosgrove*

COLOR KEY: Trick-or-Treat Party

Metallic cord	AMOUNT
■ Black	17 yds. [15.5m]

Worsted-weight	YARN AMOUNT
▨ Bt. Orange	24 yds. [21.9m]
▢ White	16 yds. [14.6m]
▨ Bt. Purple	15 yds. [13.7m]
▨ Bt. Yellow	14 yds. [12.8m]
■ Black	9 yds. [8.2m]
▨ Fern	6 yds. [5.5m]
■ Bt. Pink	4 yds. [3.7m]

STITCH KEY:
- ⊟ Backstitch/Straight

Treat Totes

*These three quick-and-easy Halloween totes are irresistible not only because
they are fun, but also because they require minimal stitching for last minute take-alongs.*

SIZE
Each Tote is 2¼" x 10½" x 10⅞" tall [5.7cm x 26.7cm x 27.6cm].

SKILL LEVEL: Challenging

MATERIALS FOR ONE OF EACH
- Four sheets of purple 7-mesh plastic canvas
- Three sheets each of black and white 7-mesh plastic canvas
- ½ sheet of orange 7-mesh plastic canvas
- ¼ sheet of lt. green 7-mesh plastic canvas
- Craft glue or glue gun
- Metallic cord; for amounts see individual Color Keys on pages 131-133.

CAT TOTE
CUTTING INSTRUCTIONS
   A: For Cat Tote Sides, cut two from purple according to graph.

   B: For Cat Tote End pieces and Bottom, from white, cut four 7w x 55h-holes for End pieces and one 70w x 14h-holes for Bottom (no graphs).

   C: For Cat Body, cut one from black according to graph.

   D: For Cat Head, cut one from black according to graph.

   E: For Cat Nose, cut one from purple according to graph.

   F: For Cat Eye Inset, cut one from lt. green according to graph.

   G: For Pumpkin, cut one from orange according to graph.

   H: For Pumpkin Stem, cut one from lt. green according to graph.

STITCHING INSTRUCTIONS
NOTE: One A and B pieces are not worked.

1: Positioning C on one A as indicated on graph, using white/silver and stitches indicated, work through both thicknesses as one according to C graph.

2: Positioning E on one side and F on opposite side of D as indicated (see photo), using white/silver and stitches indicated, work through all thicknesses according to E graph. Positioning head assembly on A as indicated, using white/silver and sitches indicated, work through all thicknesses as one as needed according to D graph.

3: Positioning G and H pieces on A as indicated (see photo), using red/orange/gold and stitches indicated, work through all thicknesses as one according to G graph.

4: With white/silver, whipstitch A and B pieces together in every other hole (see photo) according to Tote Assembly Illustration on page 130; do not overcast unfinished edges.

GHOST TOTE
CUTTING INSTRUCTIONS
   A: For Ghost Tote Sides, cut two from black according to graph.

   B: For Ghost Tote End pieces and Bottom, from purple, cut four 7w x 51h-holes for End pieces and one 70w x 14h-holes for Bottom (no graphs).

   C: For Ghost Body, cut one from white according to graph.

   D: For Ghost Arm, cut one from white according to graph.

   E: For Ghost Facial Inset, cut one from purple according to graph.

   F and G: Follow Steps G and H of Cat Tote.

STITCHING INSTRUCTIONS
NOTE: One A and B pieces are not worked.

1: Positioning C on one A with E between as indicated on graph, using purple/silver and stitches indicated, work through all thicknesses as one according to C graph.

2: Using purple/silver and stitches indicated, work D according to graph, positioning D on A and working through both thicknesses between ▲ and between ♦ symbols as you work as indicated.

3: Substituting F for G and G for H, follow Step 3 of Cat Tote.

4: Substituting purple/silver for white/silver, follow Step 4 of Cat Tote.

BOO TOTE
CUTTING INSTRUCTIONS
A: For Boo Tote Sides, cut two from white according to graph.

B: For Boo Tote End pieces and Bottom, from black, cut four 7w x 55h-holes for End pieces and one 70w x 14h-holes for Bottom (no graphs).

C: For Boo Letters, cut one each from purple according to graphs.

D: For Boo Pupils, cut two from black according to graph.

E and F: Follow Steps G and H of Cat Tote.

STITCHING INSTRUCTIONS
1: Positioning C and D pieces on A as indicated on graph (Overlap letters and pupils as indicated and as shown in photo.), using black/silver and stitches indicated, work through all thicknesses as one according to C graphs.

2: Substituting E for G and F for H, follow Step 3 of Cat Tote.

3: Substituting black/silver for white/silver, follow Step 4 of Cat Tote.

—Designed by Trudy Bath Smith

Tote Assembly Illustration
(Pieces are shown in different colors for contrast.)

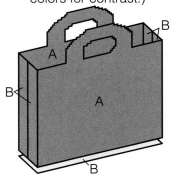

D – Cat Head
(28w x 28h-hole piece)
Cut 1 from black.

E – Cat Nose
(4w x 4h-hole piece)
Cut 1 from purple.

F – Cat Eye Inset
(13w x 13h-hole piece)
Cut 1 from lt. green.

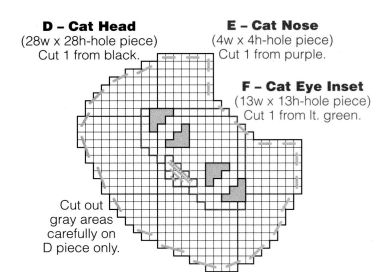

Cut out gray areas carefully on D piece only.

H – Pumpkin Stem
(6w x 7h-hole piece)
Cut 1 from lt. green.

G – Pumpkin
(22w x 17h-hole piece)
Cut 1 from orange.

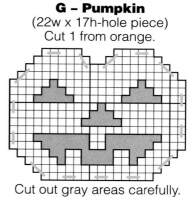

Cut out gray areas carefully.

COLOR KEY: Cat Tote

Metallic cord	AMOUNT
▨ White/Silver	10 yds. [9.1m]
▨ Red/Orange/Gold	1 yd. [0.9m]

ATTACHMENT KEY:

☐ Cat Eye Inset
☐ Head Assembly
☐ Pumpkin
☐ Pumpkin Stem

A – Cat Tote Side
(70w x 71h-hole pieces)
Cut 2 from purple.

C – Cat Body
(51w x 70h-hole piece)
Cut 1 from black.

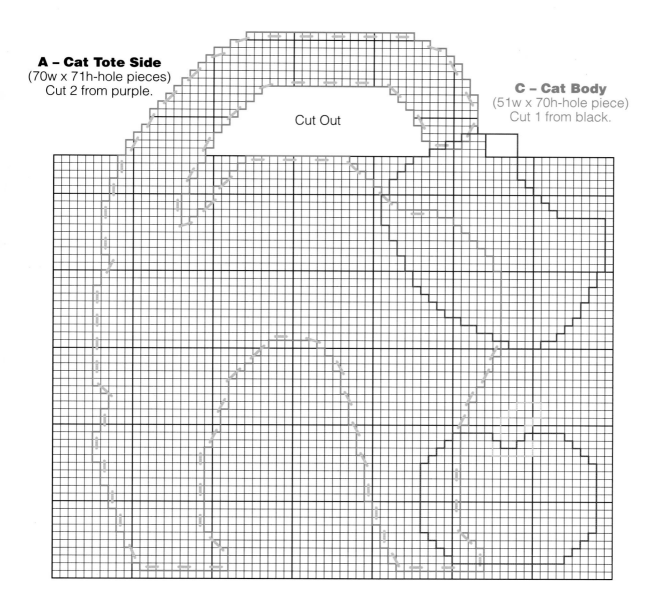

Cut Out

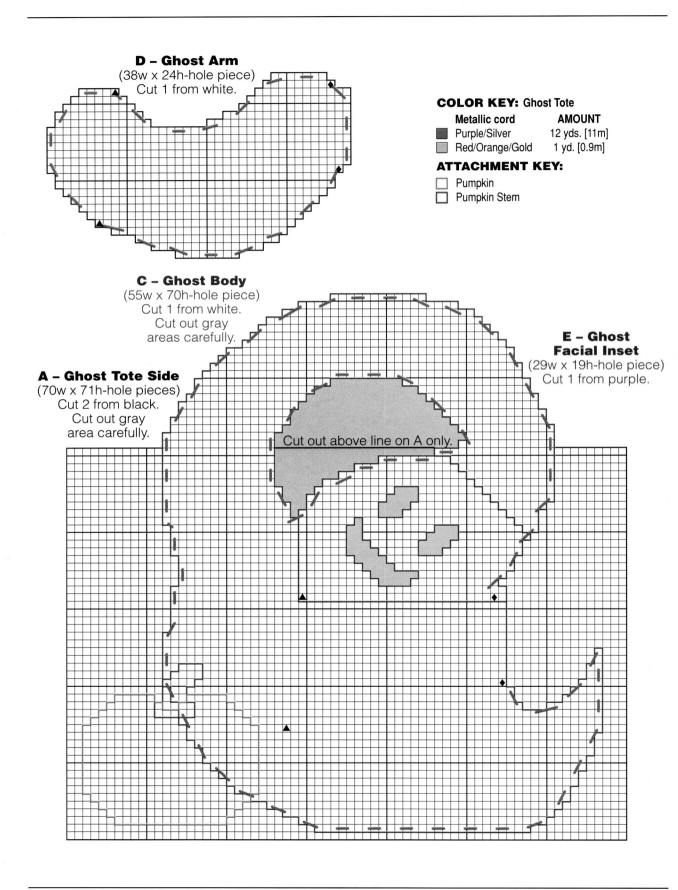

D – Ghost Arm
(38w x 24h-hole piece)
Cut 1 from white.

COLOR KEY: Ghost Tote

Metallic cord	AMOUNT
Purple/Silver	12 yds. [11m]
Red/Orange/Gold	1 yd. [0.9m]

ATTACHMENT KEY:
☐ Pumpkin
☐ Pumpkin Stem

C – Ghost Body
(55w x 70h-hole piece)
Cut 1 from white.
Cut out gray
areas carefully.

E – Ghost Facial Inset
(29w x 19h-hole piece)
Cut 1 from purple.

A – Ghost Tote Side
(70w x 71h-hole pieces)
Cut 2 from black.
Cut out gray
area carefully.

Cut out above line on A only.

D – Boo Pupil
(9w x 16h-hole pieces)
Cut 2 from black.

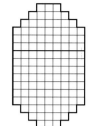

COLOR KEY: Boo Tote

Metallic cord	AMOUNT
■ Black/Silver	10 yds. [9.1m]
▨ Red/Orange/Gold	1 yd. [0.9m]

ATTACHMENT KEY:
- ☐ Pupil
- ☐ Pumpkin
- ☐ Pumpkin Stem

C – Boo Letter "B"
(39w x 38h-hole piece)
Cut 1 from purple.

C – Boo Letter "O" #1
(29w x 32h-hole piece)
Cut 1 from purple.
Cut out gray area carefully.

C – Boo Letter "O" #2
(29w x 32h-hole piece)
Cut 1 from purple.
Cut out gray area
carefully.

A – Boo Tote Side
(70w x 71h-hole pieces)
Cut 2 from white.

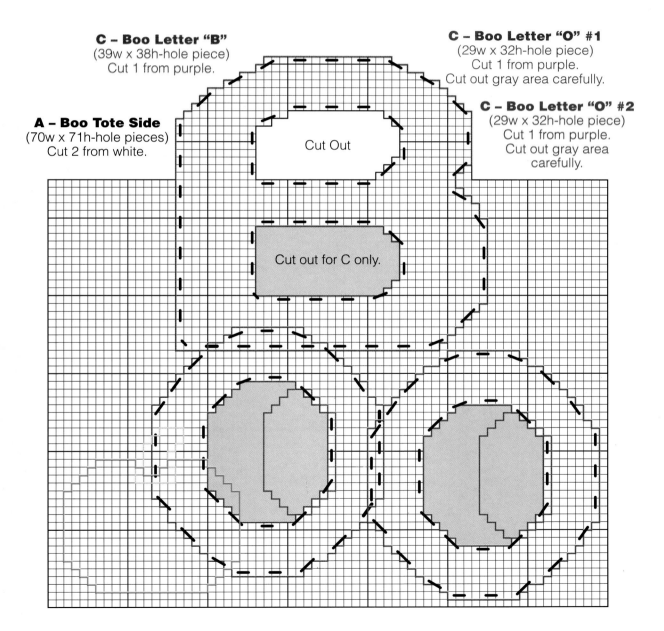

Cut Out

Cut out for C only.

SCARY SNEEZES

*Add some creepy characters to your holiday
decorating with these three boutique tissue box covers.*

SIZE
Each snugly covers a boutique-style tissue box.

SKILL LEVEL: Average

MATERIALS
- Five sheets of 7-mesh plastic canvas
- Scrap of red 7-mesh plastic canvas
- One black 12" [30.5cm] chenille stem
- Craft glue or glue gun
- Worsted-weight or plastic canvas yarn; for amounts see individual Color Keys on pages 136 and 137.

CUTTING INSTRUCTIONS
NOTE: Use red canvas for N and clear canvas for remaining pieces.

A: For Cover Tops, cut three according to graph.

B: For Cover Sides, cut twelve 30w x 36h-holes (no graph).

C: For Pumpkin Eyes, Nose and Mouth, cut number indicated according to graphs.

D: For Pumpkin Stem, cut one according to graph.

E: For Pumpkin Leaf, cut one according to graph.

F: For Kitty Eyes, Nose and Muzzle, cut number indicated according to graphs.

G: For Kitty Ears #1 and #2, cut one each according to graphs.

H: For Kitty Tail, cut one according to graph.

I: For Kitty Hat, cut one according to graph.

J: For Kitty Bow Tie, cut one according to graph.

K: For Monster Eyes and Nose, cut number indicated according to graphs.

L: For Monster Ears #1 and #2, cut one each according to graphs.

M: For Monster Hair Sides, cut four according to graph.

N: For Monster Mouth, cut one from red according to graph.

O: For Monster Bolt Ends, cut two according to graph.

P: For Monster Bolt Sides, cut two 13w x 7h-holes (no graph).

STITCHING INSTRUCTIONS
NOTE: N is not worked.

1: Using colors and stitches indicated, work A, C-M and O pieces according to graphs; using black, bright green and orange and slanted gobelin stitch over five bars, work four B pieces in each color in horizontal rows (see photo). Using gray and continental stitch, work P pieces. With matching colors, overcast cutout edges of A and outer edges of C, D, F-L and O pieces.

2: For each Cover (make 3), with matching color, whipstitch corresponding A and B pieces wrong sides together; overcast unfinished edges. With dark green, whipstitch X edges of E wrong sides together as indicated; overcast unfinished edges. With black, whipstitch M pieces wrong sides together as indicated; overcast unfinished edges.

NOTE: Cut two 1¼" [3.2cm] lengths of black.

3: Wrap one cut strand around each Kitty Eye as shown in photo; glue to secure. For each Monster Bolt (make 2), with gray, whipstitch and assemble one of each O and P pieces according to Bolt Assembly Diagram on page 137.

4: For each Cover, glue corresponding pieces to Cover as indicated and as shown in photo. Wrap chenille stem around a pencil to curl; glue curls to Pumpkin Cover as shown.

—Designed by Sandra Miller Maxfield

A – Cover Top
(30w x 30h-hole pieces)
Cut 3. Work 1; substituting
black for orange, work 2.

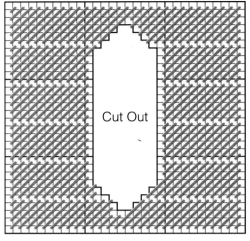

Cut Out

H – Kitty Tail
(25w x 12h-hole piece)
Cut 1 & work.

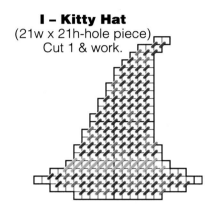

Glue to cover.

I – Kitty Hat
(21w x 21h-hole piece)
Cut 1 & work.

F – Kitty Eye
(5w x 5h-hole pieces)
Cut 2 & work.

F – Kitty Nose
(9w x 6h-hole piece)
Cut 1 & work.

F – Kitty Muzzle
(19w x 18h-hole piece)
Cut 1 & work.

J – Kitty Bow Tie
(16w x 16h-hole piece)
Cut 1 & work.

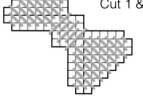

COLOR KEY: Kitty Cover

Worsted-weight	YARN AMOUNT
■ Black	3 oz. [85g]
▨ White	10 yds. [9.1m]
▨ Purple	8 yds. [7.3m]
▨ Bright Green	6 yds. [5.5m]
▨ Orange	3 yds. [2.7m]
▨ Pink	3 yds. [2.7m]

G – Kitty Ear #1
(14w x 13h-hole piece)
Cut 1 & work.

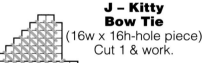

Glue to cover.

G – Kitty Ear #2
(14w x 13h-hole piece)
Cut 1 & work.

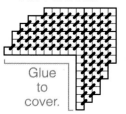

Glue to cover.

D – Pumpkin Stem
(13w x 10h-hole piece)
Cut 1 & work.

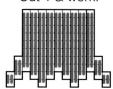

COLOR KEY: Pumpkin Cover

Worsted-weight		YARN AMOUNT
	Orange	3 oz. [85g]
	Black	6 yds. [5.5m]
	Dark Green	4 yds. [3.7m]
	Maple	3 yds. [2.7m]

E – Pumpkin Leaf
(21w x 16h-hole piece)
Cut 1 & work.

Whipstitch X edges together.

C – Pumpkin Eye & Nose
(6w x 6h-hole pieces)
Cut 3. Work 1 for Nose &
2 for Eyes.

C – Pumpkin Mouth
(24w x 9h-hole piece)
Cut 1 & work.

K – Monster Nose
(10w x 8h-hole piece)
Cut 1 & work.

K – Monster Eye
(7w x 6h-hole pieces)
Cut 2 & work.

O – Monster Bolt End
(7w x 7h-hole pieces)
Cut 2 & work.

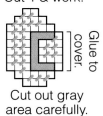

Cut out gray
area carefully.

Bolt Assembly Diagram

Step 1:
Whipstitch
ends of P
together;
overcast
edges.

Step 2:
Glue O
& P
pieces
together.

Step 3:
Wrap P until completely
covered, securing ends
under wraps as you work.

COLOR KEY: Monster Cover

Worsted-weight		YARN AMOUNT
	Bright Green	2¹⁄₂ oz. [70.9g]
	Black	35 yds. [32m]
	Gray	10 yds. [9.1m]
	Pink	3 yds. [2.7m]
	Purple	3 yds. [2.7m]
	White	1 yd. [0.9m]

L – Monster Ear #2
(7w x 10h-hole piece)
Cut 1 & work.

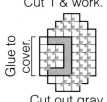

Glue to cover.

Cut out gray
area carefully.

L – Monster Ear #1
(7w x 10h-hole piece)
Cut 1 & work.

Glue to cover.

Cut out gray
area carefully.

M – Monster Hair Side
(31w x 8h-hole pieces) Cut 4 & work.

Whipstitch

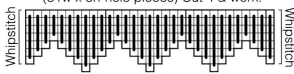

Whipstitch

N – Monster Mouth
(20w x 4h-hole piece)
Cut 1 from red.

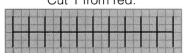

Cut around bars carefully.

AUTUMN SPLENDOR

*Fill your home with these fantastic fall
accessories, including a wreath, basket and table trimmings.*

SIZES
Basket is 8¼" across x 5⅛" tall [21cm x 13cm], not including handle; Place Mat is 12" x 18" [30.5cm x 45.7cm]; Wreath is 18" across [45.7cm]; Napkin Ring is 2" x 2¾" x 3⅛" [5.1cm x 7cm x 7.9cm].

SKILL LEVEL: Average

MATERIALS
- One ivory plastic canvas oval place mat
- One 9½" [24.1cm] plastic canvas radial circle
- 1¼ sheets of ivory 7-mesh plastic canvas
- 1½ sheet each of yellow, brown, orange, burgundy and red 7-mesh plastic canvas
- ¼ sheet of peach 7-mesh plastic canvas
- One sheet of orange 10-mesh plastic canvas
- One 18" [45.7cm] straw wreath
- 5½ yds. [5m] of harvest print 2½" [6.4cm] wire-edged floral ribbon
- Iron
- One cluster of artificial seasonal novelties
- Craft glue or glue gun
- Worsted-weight or plastic canvas yarn; for amounts see Color Key on page 140.

CUTTING INSTRUCTIONS
NOTE: Use 7-mesh for A-D pieces and 10-mesh canvas for G and H pieces.

A: For Maple Leaves, cut eleven (two each from yellow, brown, orange, burgundy and red and one from peach) according to graph.

B: For Oak Leaves, cut six (one each from yellow, brown, orange, burgundy, red and peach) according to graph.

C: For Basket Side Pieces, cut two from ivory according to graph.

D: For Basket Handle, cut one from ivory according to graph.

E: For Basket Bottom, cut away outer five rows of holes from circle to measure 7¾"

[19.7cm] across (no graph).

F: For Place Mat, use oval place mat (no graph).

G: For Napkin Ring Leaf, cut one from orange 10-mesh according to A graph.

H: For Napkin Ring Band, cut one from orange 10-mesh 58w x 10h-holes (no graph).

STITCHING INSTRUCTIONS
NOTE: D-F and H pieces are not worked.

1: Using tangerine for yellow Leaves, rust for brown Leaves, dark red for red Leaves, pumpkin for orange Leaves, dusty rose for burgundy Leaves and dark orange for peach Leaves and stitches indicated, work A and B pieces according to graphs; with matching colors, overcast edges. Set Leaves aside.

2: Using colors and stitches indicated, work C pieces according to graph. With pumpkin, overcast one long straight edge of each small cutout as indicated and edges of large cutouts on Basket Side. Whipstitch Side and E piece together; overcast unfinished top edges of Basket. Overcast edges of D, attaching one end of Handle to each side of Basket at overlapped area as you work.

NOTE: Cut one 27" [68.6cm] and two 9" [22.9cm] lengths of ribbon.

3: With ends on inside, weave 27" [68.6cm] ribbon through cutouts on Basket Side as shown in photo; glue ends of ribbon together to secure. Glue four Maple Leaves of choice to Basket as shown. For each Handle tie (make 2), with iron set on low heat, assemble one 9" [22.9cm] length of ribbon according to Handle Tie Folding Diagram on page 140. Wrap tie around one Handle end as shown and glue to secure.

4: For Place Mat, with pumpkin, overcast edges of F. Glue one Oak and two Maple Leaves of choice to Place Mat as shown or as desired.

NOTE: Cut one 2½-yd. [2.3m] length of ribbon.

5: For Wreath, wrap 2½-yd. ribbon around straw wreath; glue ends to wreath to secure. Tie remaining ribbon into a decorative bow.

Glue bow, cluster of seasonal novelties and remaining A and B pieces to wreath (see photo).

6: For Napkin Ring, using pumpkin for Leaf color and stitches indicated, work G according to A graph; overcast edges. Overlapping ends of H three holes, whipstitch together; overcast unfinished edges. Glue Leaf to Band as shown.

—Designed by Glenda Chamberlain

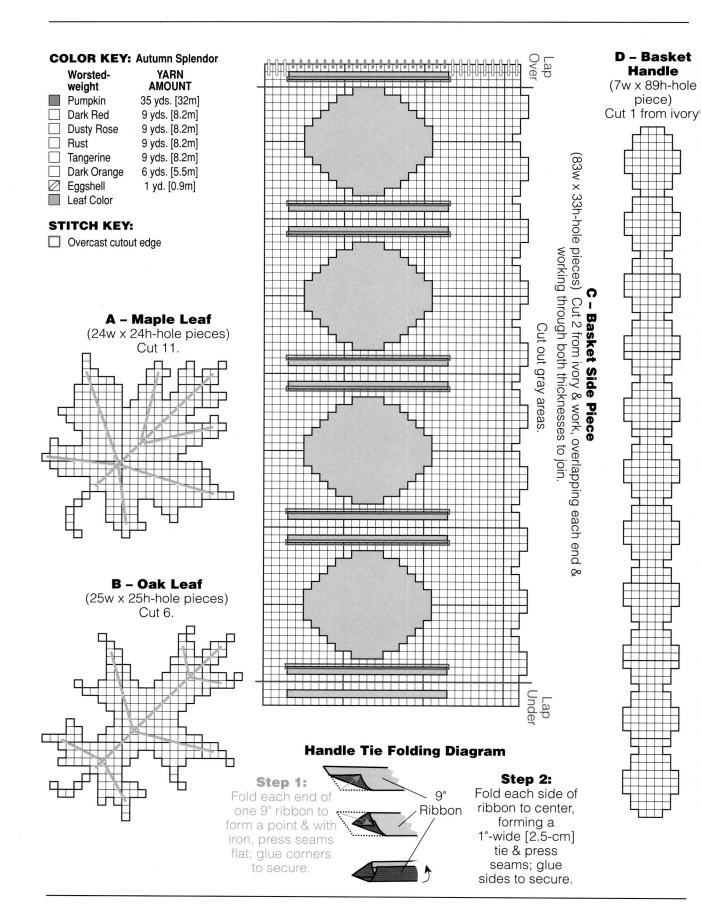

COLOR KEY: Autumn Splendor

Worsted-weight		YARN AMOUNT
▨	Pumpkin	35 yds. [32m]
☐	Dark Red	9 yds. [8.2m]
☐	Dusty Rose	9 yds. [8.2m]
☐	Rust	9 yds. [8.2m]
☐	Tangerine	9 yds. [8.2m]
☐	Dark Orange	6 yds. [5.5m]
▨	Eggshell	1 yd. [0.9m]
▦	Leaf Color	

STITCH KEY:

☐ Overcast cutout edge

A – Maple Leaf
(24w x 24h-hole pieces)
Cut 11.

B – Oak Leaf
(25w x 25h-hole pieces)
Cut 6.

Lap Over

Lap Under

(83w x 33h-hole pieces) Cut 2 from ivory & work, overlapping each end & working through both thicknesses to join.

Cut out gray areas.

C – Basket Side Piece

D – Basket Handle
(7w x 89h-hole piece)
Cut 1 from ivory

Handle Tie Folding Diagram

Step 1:
Fold each end of one 9" ribbon to form a point & with iron, press seams flat; glue corners to secure.

9" Ribbon

Step 2:
Fold each side of ribbon to center, forming a 1"-wide [2.5-cm] tie & press seams; glue sides to secure.

PROUD TOM TURKEY

Top your Thanksgiving table with this stately Tom Turkey.

SIZE
7" x 7" x 7½" tall [17.8cm x 17.8cm x 19cm].

SKILL LEVEL: Average

MATERIALS
- Five sheets of 7-mesh plastic canvas
- Polyester fiberfill
- Craft glue or glue gun
- Worsted-weight or plastic canvas yarn; for amounts see Color Key on page 142.

CUTTING INSTRUCTIONS

A: For Turkey Sides #1 and #2, cut one each according to graphs.

B: For Turkey Front, cut one according to graph.

C: For Turkey Wings #1 and #2, cut one each according to graphs.

D: For Turkey Back, cut one according to graph.

E: For Turkey Bottom, cut one according to graph.

F: For Turkey Tail, cut one according to graph.

G: For Base, cut one according to graph.

H: For Leaves, cut nine according to graph.

STITCHING INSTRUCTIONS

1: Using colors and stitches indicated, work A, C, F, G and H according to graphs. Fill in uncoded areas of A, C and F and work B, D and E pieces using dark rust and continental stitch. With black for wing tips and with matching colors, overcast edges of C, F, G and H pieces.

2: Using black and embroidery stitches indicated, embroider detail on C and F pieces as indicated on graphs.

3: With matching colors, whipstitch A, B, D and E pieces wrong sides together as indicated and according to Turkey Assembly Illustration, stuffing with fiberfill before closing.

4: Glue one Wing to each side of Turkey and Turkey to center of Base; glue Tail to back of Turkey (see photo). Glue Leaves to Base as desired.

—*Designed by Judy Nelson*

H – Leaf
(12w x 15h-hole pieces)
Cut 9. Work 2 & 1 reversed; substituting dark rust, camel & rust for yellow, work 1 & 1 reversed in each color.

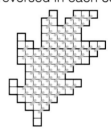

B – Turkey Front
(15w x 12h-hole piece)
Cut 1 & work.

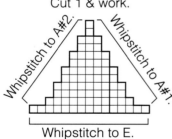

Whipstitch to A#2.

Whipstitch to A#1.

Whipstitch to E.

Turkey Assembly Illustration
(Gray denotes wrong side.)

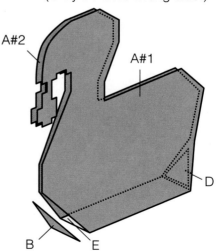

A#2

A#1

D

B

E

COLOR KEY: Proud Tom Turkey

Worsted-weight	YARN AMOUNT
☐ Dark Rust	47 yds. [43m]
■ Forest	40 yds. [36.6m]
■ Camel	15 yds. [13.7m]
■ Sand	11 yds. [10.1m]
■ Black	9 yds. [8.2m]
■ Dark Brown	7 yds. [6.4m]
☐ Yellow	7 yds. [6.4m]
☐ Rust	4 yds. [3.7m]
■ Red	1 yd. [0.9m]

STITCH KEY:

⊟ Backstitch/Straight

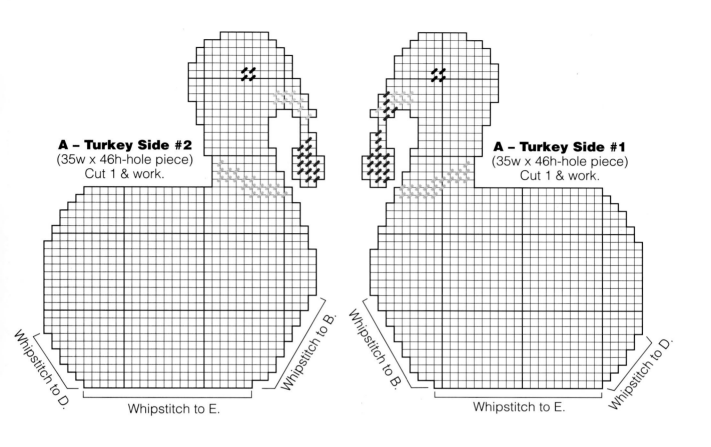

A – Turkey Side #2
(35w x 46h-hole piece)
Cut 1 & work.

A – Turkey Side #1
(35w x 46h-hole piece)
Cut 1 & work.

Whipstitch to D.

Whipstitch to B.

Whipstitch to E.

Whipstitch to B.

Whipstitch to E.

Whipstitch to D.

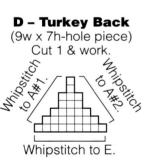

D – Turkey Back
(9w x 7h-hole piece)
Cut 1 & work.

Whipstitch to A #1.

Whipstitch to A #2.

Whipstitch to E.

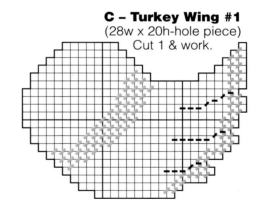

C – Turkey Wing #1
(28w x 20h-hole piece)
Cut 1 & work.

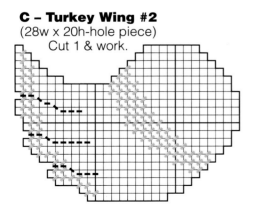

C – Turkey Wing #2
(28w x 20h-hole piece)
Cut 1 & work.

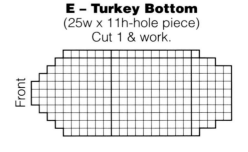

E – Turkey Bottom
(25w x 11h-hole piece)
Cut 1 & work.

Front

F – Tail
(48w x 48h-hole piece)
Cut 1 & work.

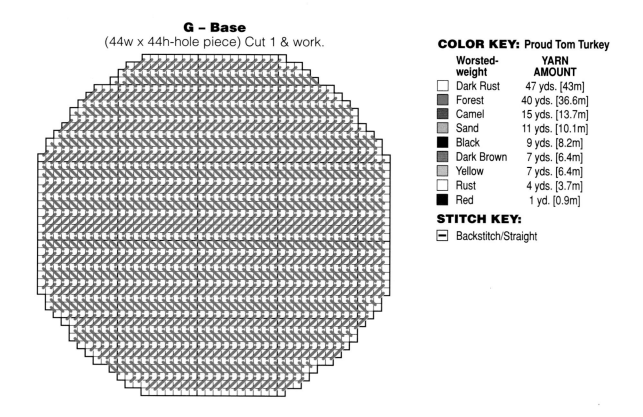

G – Base
(44w x 44h-hole piece) Cut 1 & work.

COLOR KEY: Proud Tom Turkey

Worsted-weight		YARN AMOUNT
☐	Dark Rust	47 yds. [43m]
▨	Forest	40 yds. [36.6m]
▨	Camel	15 yds. [13.7m]
▨	Sand	11 yds. [10.1m]
■	Black	9 yds. [8.2m]
▨	Dark Brown	7 yds. [6.4m]
▨	Yellow	7 yds. [6.4m]
☐	Rust	4 yds. [3.7m]
■	Red	1 yd. [0.9m]

STITCH KEY:

⊟ Backstitch/Straight

HORN OF PLENTY

Give thanks for the bountiful gifts of
nature with this grand napkin holder fit for feasting.

SIZE
2¾" x 7½" x 6⅛" tall [7cm x 19cm x 15.6cm].

SKILL LEVEL: Average

MATERIALS

- One sheet of tan 7-mesh plastic canvas
- 1½ sheets of clear 7-mesh plastic canvas
- Worsted-weight or plastic canvas yarn; for amounts see Color Key.

CUTTING INSTRUCTIONS

A: For Sides and Linings, cut four (two from clear for Sides and two from tan for Linings) according to graph.

B: For Ends, cut two from clear 17w x 13h-holes (no graph).

C: For Bottom, cut one from clear 49w x 17h-holes (no graph).

STITCHING INSTRUCTIONS

NOTE: Lining A and C pieces are not worked.

1: Using colors and stitches indicated, work clear A pieces according to graph; fill in uncoded areas and work B pieces using eggshell and continental stitch.

2: With cinnamon for cornucopia and with eggshell, whipstitch A-C pieces together according to Napkin Holder Assembly Illustration; overcast unfinished edges.

—Designed by Debby Keel

COLOR KEY: Horn of Plenty

Worsted-weight	YARN AMOUNT
☐ Eggshell	30 yds. [27.4m]
◪ Camel	12 yds. [11m]
◩ Cinnamon	12 yds. [11m]
◪ Pumpkin	6 yds. [5.5m]
■ Purple	6 yds. [5.5m]
◻ Mint	5 yds. [4.6m]
◪ Maple	4 yds. [3.7m]
■ Dark Brown	2 yds. [1.8m]
■ Dark Red	2 yds. [1.8m]
◪ Lavender	2 yds. [1.8m]
◻ Plum	1½ yds. [1.4m]
◪ Yellow	1½ yds. [1.4m]
■ Black	1 yd. [0.9m]
■ Forest	1 yd. [0.9m]
◻ Straw	1 yd. [0.9m]

Napkin Holder Assembly Illustration
(Pieces are shown in different colors for contrast; gray denotes wrong side.)

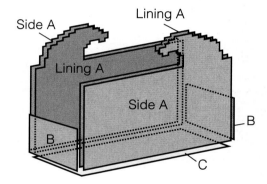

A – Side & Lining
(49w x 40h-hole pieces)
Cut 2 from clear for Sides & work.
Cut 2 from tan for Linings & leave unworked.

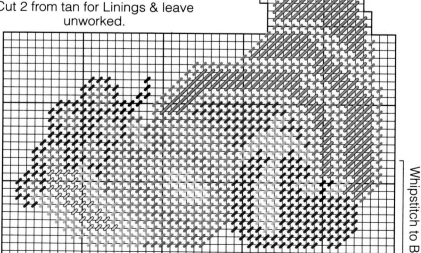

Whipstitch to B.

Whipstitch to B.

FROSTED POINSETTIAS

*Celebrate the spirit of winter with sparkling
table accessories including a place mat, napkin rings and a goodie holder.*

SIZES

Place Mat is 11¼" x 16½" [28.6cm x 41.9cm]; Napkin Ring is 1½" x 2" [3.8cm x 5.1cm] not including motif; Basket is 6" across x 4" tall [15.2cm x 10.2cm].

SKILL LEVEL: Average

MATERIALS

- One white 12" x 18" [30.5cm x 45.7cm] or larger sheet of 7-mesh plastic canvas
- ½ sheet of white 7-mesh plastic canvas
- One 5" [12.7cm] plastic canvas hexagon shape
- Two sheets of pink 12" x 18" [30.5cm x 45.7cm] craft foam
- Craft glue or glue gun
- Metallic cord; for amounts see Color Key.

CUTTING INSTRUCTIONS

A: For Place Mat, cut one from large sheet according to graph.

B: For Napkin Ring Band, cut one according to graph.

C: For Napkin Ring Motif, cut one 15w x 15h-holes.

D: For Basket Sides, cut six according to graph.

E: For Basket Bottom, use hexagon shape (no graph).

STITCHING INSTRUCTIONS

NOTE: E is not worked.

1: Using colors and stitches indicated and leaving uncoded areas unworked, work A-D pieces according to graphs. With green, overcast edges of C.

2: Using white/gold and French knot, embroider detail on A and C pieces as indicated on graphs.

NOTE: Cut one 11¼" x 16½" [28.6cm x 41.9cm] piece and one 1½" x 7¼" [3.8cm x 18.4cm] strip of foam.

3: Glue large foam piece to back of Place Mat as shown in photo. For Napkin Ring, overlap short ends of foam strip; glue strip to inside and Motif to outside of Band at overlapped area.

NOTE: Cut six 3¼" x 3¾" [8.2cm x 9.5cm] pieces of foam.

4: With white/silver, whipstitch D and E pieces together as indicated, forming Basket. Glue foam pieces inside Basket sides as shown.

—Designed by
Glenda Chamberlain

C – Napkin Ring Motif
(15w x 15h-hole piece)
Cut 1 & work.

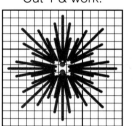

D – Basket Side
(24w x 25h-hole pieces) Cut 6 & work.
Cut out gray areas.

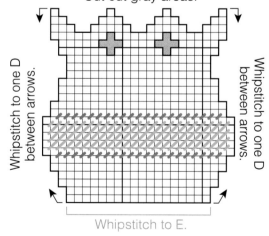

Whipstitch to one D between arrows.

Whipstitch to one D between arrows.

Whipstitch to E.

COLOR KEY: Frosted Poinsettias

Metallic cord	AMOUNT
White/Silver	20 yds. [18.3m]
Green	14 yds. [12.8m]
Magenta	5 yds. [4.6m]
White/Gold	1 yd. [0.9m]

STITCH KEY:
- ● French Knot

B – Napkin Ring Band (44w x 9h-hole piece) Cut 1 & work, overlapping ends & working through both thicknesses at overlap area to join.
Cut out gray areas.

Lap
Over

Lap
Under

A – Place Mat (109w x 74h-hole piece) Cut 1 from large sheet & work. Cut out gray areas.

Classic St. Nick

This classic Santa makes a great tree topper, air freshener cover or even a gift.

SIZE
4½" across x about 11¼" tall [11.4cm x 28.6cm].

SKILL LEVEL: Average

MATERIALS
- One sheet of 7-mesh plastic canvas
- One white 1½" [3.8cm] pom-pom
- Craft glue or glue gun
- Metallic cord; for amount see Color Key.
- Worsted-weight or plastic canvas yarn; for amounts see Color Key.

CUTTING INSTRUCTIONS
  A: For Body, cut one according to graph.
  B: For Arms, cut two according to graph.
  C: For Beard, cut one according to graph.
  D: For Mustache, cut one according to graph.

STITCHING INSTRUCTIONS
1: Using colors and stitches indicated, work A-C pieces according to graphs.

2: Using colors and embroidery stitches indicated, embroider detail on A as indicated.

3: Folding Body wrong sides together, with matching colors, whipstitch A together as indicated; overcast unfinished edges. With white for mustache and with matching colors, overcast unfinished edges of B-D pieces.

4: Glue pom-pom to top of hat and Beard, Mustache and Arms to Body as shown in photo.
—*Designed by Fran Rohus*

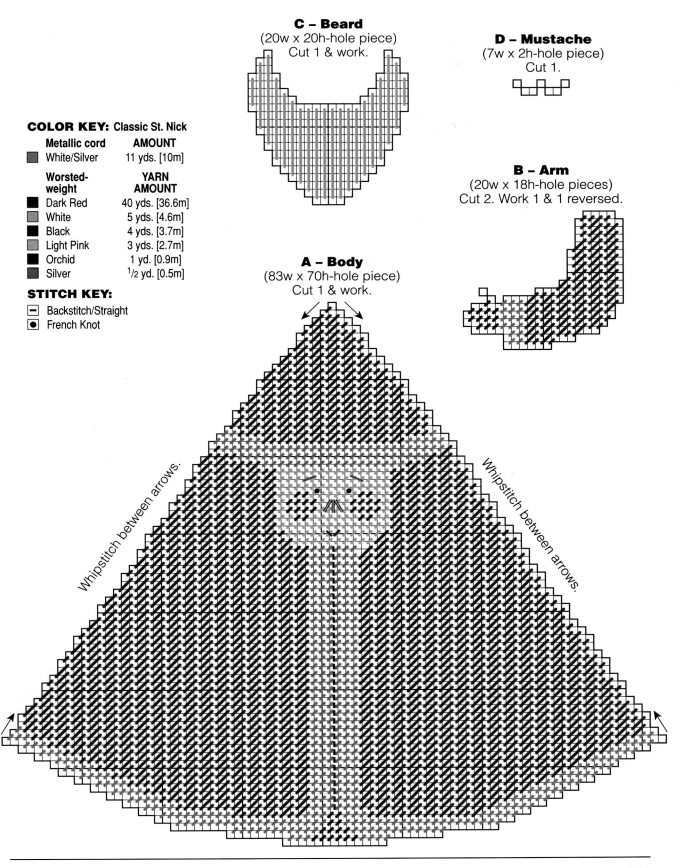

C – Beard
(20w x 20h-hole piece)
Cut 1 & work.

D – Mustache
(7w x 2h-hole piece)
Cut 1.

COLOR KEY: Classic St. Nick

Metallic cord	AMOUNT
White/Silver	11 yds. [10m]

Worsted-weight	YARN AMOUNT
Dark Red	40 yds. [36.6m]
White	5 yds. [4.6m]
Black	4 yds. [3.7m]
Light Pink	3 yds. [2.7m]
Orchid	1 yd. [0.9m]
Silver	1/2 yd. [0.5m]

STITCH KEY:
- ▬ Backstitch/Straight
- ⊙ French Knot

B – Arm
(20w x 18h-hole pieces)
Cut 2. Work 1 & 1 reversed.

A – Body
(83w x 70h-hole piece)
Cut 1 & work.

Whipstitch between arrows.

Whipstitch between arrows.

HOLIDAY HUGGERS

These two cheerful holiday characters are here
to hold treats and seasonal cards for friends and family to enjoy.

SIZE
Each is about 4¼" x 9½" x 12½" tall [10.8cm x 24.1cm x 31.8cm].

SKILL LEVEL: Average

MATERIALS
- Two sheets each of red, white and clear 7-mesh plastic canvas
- Six red 3mm faceted beads
- Two 20mm black, three 17mm red and one 10mm blue button
- ½ yd. [0.5m] of metallic plaid 1¼" [3.2cm] ribbon
- Craft glue or glue gun
- Metallic cord; for amounts see individual Color Keys on pages 154 and 155.
- Worsted-weight or plastic canvas yarn; for amounts see individual Color Keys.

SANTA HUGGER
CUTTING INSTRUCTIONS
A: For Front and Lining, cut two (one from clear for Front and one from red for Lining) according to graph.

B: For Back and Backing, cut two (one from clear for Back and one from red for Backing) according to graph.

C: For Sides and Linings, cut four (two from clear for Sides and two from red for Linings) 27w x 13h-holes (no graph).

D: For Bottom, cut one from clear 62w x 27h-holes (no graph).

E: For Holly Leaf, cut one from clear according to graph.

STITCHING INSTRUCTIONS
NOTE: Lining A, Backing B, Lining C and D pieces are not worked.

1: Using colors and stitches indicated, work clear A for Front, clear B for Back and E pieces according to graphs. Using red and continental stitch, work clear C pieces for Sides. With gold cord, overcast edges of E.

2: Using cord colors and embroidery stitches indicated, embroider detail on Front A, Back B and E pieces as indicated on graphs.

3: With matching colors, whipstitch A-D pieces together as indicated and according to Basket Assembly Illustration.

4: Glue Holly Leaf to hat and red beads to Holly Leaf as shown in photo.

SNOWMAN HUGGER
CUTTING INSTRUCTIONS
A: For Front and Lining, cut two (one from clear for Front and one from white for Lining) according to graph.

B: For Back and Backing, cut two (one from clear for Back and one from white for Backing) according to graph.

C-E: Substituting white for red, follow Steps C-E of Santa Hugger.

STITCHING INSTRUCTIONS
NOTE: Lining A, Backing B, Lining C and D pieces are not worked.

1: Substituting white for red on C pieces, follow Step 1 of Santa Hugger.

2: Using yarn and cord in colors and embroidery stitches indicated, embroider detail on Front A, Back B and E pieces as indicated on graphs.

3-4: Follow Steps 3 and 4 of Santa Hugger.

5: Glue buttons to Back A as indicated. Wrap ribbon around neck and tie into a bow as shown.

—*Designed by Debby Keel*

Basket Assembly Illustration
(Gray denotes wrong side.)

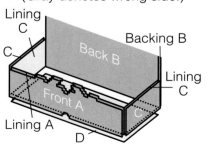

A – Santa Hugger Front & Lining
(62w x 16h-hole pieces)
Cut 1 from clear for Front & work. Cut 1 from red for Lining & leave unworked.

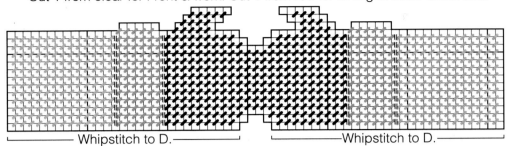

├── Whipstitch to D. ──┤ ├── Whipstitch to D. ──┤

B – Santa Hugger
Back & Backing
(62w x 82h-hole pieces)
Cut 1 from clear for Back & work.
Cut 1 from red for Backing &
leave unworked.

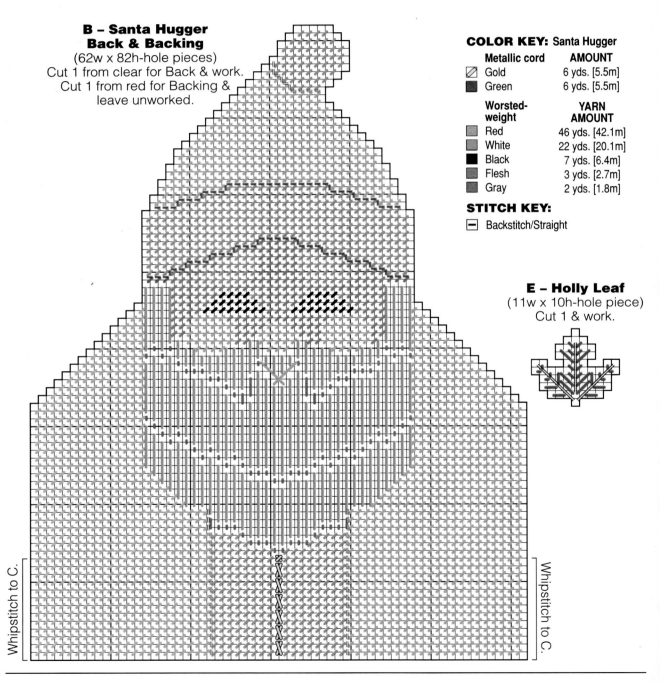

COLOR KEY: Santa Hugger

Metallic cord	AMOUNT
Gold	6 yds. [5.5m]
Green	6 yds. [5.5m]

Worsted-weight	YARN AMOUNT
Red	46 yds. [42.1m]
White	22 yds. [20.1m]
Black	7 yds. [6.4m]
Flesh	3 yds. [2.7m]
Gray	2 yds. [1.8m]

STITCH KEY:

▬ Backstitch/Straight

E – Holly Leaf
(11w x 10h-hole piece)
Cut 1 & work.

Whipstitch to C.

Whipstitch to C.

A – Snowman Hugger Front & Lining
(62w x 16h-hole pieces)
Cut 1 from clear for Front & work.
Cut 1 from white for Lining & leave unworked.

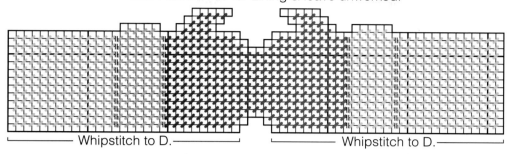

Whipstitch to D. ———— Whipstitch to D.

B – Snowman Hugger Back & Backing
(62w x 82h-hole pieces)
Cut 1 from clear for
Back & work.
Cut 1 from white for
Backing & leave unworked.

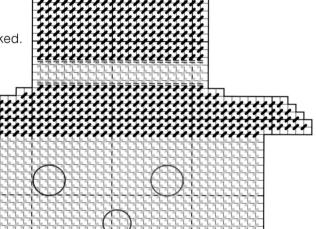

COLOR KEY: Snowman Hugger

Metallic cord	AMOUNT
Gold	6 yds. [5.5m]
Green	1½ yds. [1.4m]

Worsted-weight	YARN AMOUNT
White	50 yds. [45.7m]
Black	11 yds. [10.1m]
Green	6 yds. [5.5m]
Royal	6 yds. [5.5m]
Red	4 yds. [3.7m]

STITCH KEY:

⊟ Backstitch/Straight

PLACEMENT KEY:

◘ Black Button
◘ Blue Button
◘ Red Button

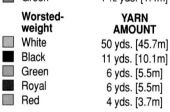

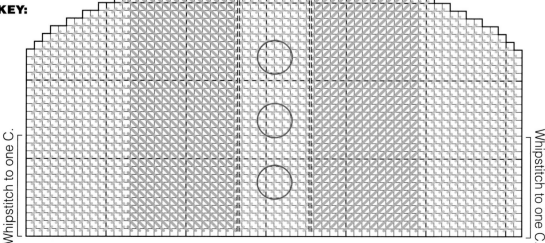

Whipstitch to one C.

Whipstitch to one C.

READY, SET, STITCH

Get ready to stitch like a pro
with these simple, step-by-step guidelines.

GETTING STARTED

Most plastic canvas stitchers love getting their projects organized before they even step out the door in search of supplies. A few moments of careful planning can make the creation of your project even more fun.

First of all, prepare your work area. You will need a flat surface for cutting and assembly, and you will need a place to store your materials. Good lighting is essential, and a comfortable chair will make your stitching time even more enjoyable.

Do you plan to make one project, or will you be making several of the same item? A materials list appears at the beginning of each pattern. If you plan to make several of the same item, multiply your materials accordingly. Your shopping list is ready.

CHOOSING CANVAS

Most projects can be made using standard-size sheets of canvas. Standard size sheets of 7-mesh (7 holes per inch) are always 70 x 90 holes and are about 10½" x 13½" [26.7cm x 34.3cm]. For larger projects, 7-mesh canvas also comes in 12" x 18" [30.5cm x 45.7cm],

which is always 80 x 120 holes and 13½" x 22½" [34.3cm x 57.2cm], which is always 90 x 150 holes. Other shapes are available in 7-mesh, including circles, diamonds, purse forms and ovals.

10-mesh canvas (10 holes per inch) comes only in standard-size sheets, which vary slightly depending on brand. They are 10½" x 13½" [26.7cm x 34.3cm], which is always 106 x 136 holes or 11" x 14" [27.9cm x 35.6cm], which is always 108 x 138 holes.

5-mesh canvas (5 holes per inch) and 14-mesh (14 holes per inch) sheets are also available.

Some canvas is soft and pliable, while other canvas is stiffer and more rigid. To prevent canvas from cracking during or after stitching, you'll want to choose pliable canvas for projects that require shaping, like round baskets with curved handles. For easier shaping, warm canvas pieces with a blow-dry hair dryer to soften; dip in cool water to set. If your project is a box or an item that will stand alone, stiffer canvas is more suitable.

Both 7- and 10-mesh canvas sheets are available in a rainbow of colors. Most designs can be stitched on colored as well as clear canvas. When a pattern does not specify color in the materials list, you can assume clear canvas was used in the photographed model. If you'd like to stitch only a portion of the design, leaving a portion unstitched, use colored canvas to coordinate with yarn colors.

Buy the same brand of canvas for each entire project. Different brands of canvas may differ slightly in the distance between each bar.

MARKING & COUNTING TOOLS

To avoid wasting canvas, careful cutting of each piece is important. For some pieces with square corners, you might be comfortable cutting the canvas without marking it beforehand. But for pieces with lots of angles and cutouts, you may want to mark your canvas before cutting.

Always count before you mark and cut. To count holes on the graphs, look for the bolder lines showing each ten holes. These ten-count lines begin in the lower left-hand corner of each graph and are on the graph to make counting easier. To count holes on the canvas, you may use your tapestry needle, a toothpick or a plastic hair roller pick. Insert the needle or pick slightly in each hole as you count.

Most stitchers have tried a variety of marking tools and have settled on a favorite, which may be crayon, permanent marker, grease pencil or ball point pen. One of the best marking tools is a fine-point overhead projection marker, available at office supply stores. The ink is dark and easy to see and washes off completely with water. After cutting and before stitching, it's important to remove all marks so they won't stain yarn as you stitch or show through stitches later. Cloth and paper toweling removes grease pencil and crayon marks, as do fabric softener sheets that have already been used in your dryer.

CUTTING TOOLS

You may find it helpful to have several tools on hand for cutting canvas. When cutting long, straight sections, scissors, craft cutters or kitchen shears are the fastest and easiest to use. For cutting out detailed areas and trimming nubs, you may like using manicure scissors or nail clippers. If you prefer laying your canvas flat when cutting, try a craft knife and cutting surface – self-healing mats designed for sewing and kitchen cutting boards work well.

STITCHING MATERIALS

You may choose two-ply nylon plastic canvas yarn or four-ply worsted-weight yarn for stitching on 7-mesh canvas. There are about 42 yards per ounce of plastic canvas yarn and 50 yards per ounce of worsted-weight yarn.

Worsted-weight yarn is widely available and comes in wool, acrylic, cotton and blends. If you decide to use worsted-weight yarn, choose 100% acrylic for best coverage. Select worsted-weight yarn by color instead of the color names or numbers found in the Color Keys. Projects stitched with worsted-weight yarn often "fuzz" after use. "Fuzz" can be removed by shaving it off with a  fabric shaver to make your project look new again.

Plastic canvas yarn comes in about 60 colors and is a favorite of many plastic canvas designers. These yarns "wear" well both while stitching and in the finished product. When buying plastic canvas yarn, shop using the color names or numbers found in the Color Keys, or select colors of your choice.

To cover 5-mesh canvas, use a doubled strand of worsted-weight or plastic canvas yarn.

Choose sport-weight yarn or #3 pearl cotton for stitching on 10-mesh canvas. To cover 10-mesh canvas using six-strand embroidery floss, use 12 strands held together. Single and double plies of yarn will also cover 10-mesh and can be used for embroidery or accent stitching worked over needlepoint stitches – simply separate worsted-weight yarn into 2-ply or plastic canvas yarn into 1-ply. Nylon plastic canvas yarn does not perform as well as knitting worsted when separated and can be frustrating to use, but it is possible. Just use short lengths, separate into single plies and twist each ply slightly.

Embroidery floss or #5 pearl cotton can also be used for embroidery, and each covers 14-mesh canvas well.

Metallic cord is a tightly-woven cord that comes in dozens of glittering colors. Some are solid-color metallics, including gold and silver, and some have colors interwoven with gold or silver threads. If your metallic cord has a white core, the core may be removed for super-easy stitching. To do so, cut a length of cord; grasp center core fibers with tweezers or fingertips and pull. Core slips out easily. Though the sparkly look of metallics will add much to your project, you may substitute contrasting colors of yarn.

Natural and synthetic raffia straw will cover 7-mesh canvas if flattened before stitching. Use short lengths to prevent splitting, and glue ends to prevent unraveling.

CUTTING CANVAS

Follow all Cutting Instructions, Notes and labels above graphs to cut canvas. Each piece is labeled with a letter of the alphabet. Square-sided pieces are cut according to hole count, and some may not have a graph.

Unlike sewing patterns, graphs are not designed to be used as actual patterns but rather as counting, cutting and stitching guides. Therefore, graphs may not be actual size. Count the holes on the graph (see Marking & Counting Tools), mark your canvas to match, then cut. The old carpenters' adage – "Measure twice, cut once" – is good advice. Trim off the nubs close to the bar, and trim all corners diagonally.

For large projects, as you cut each piece, it is a good idea to label it with its letter and name. Use sticky labels, or fasten scrap paper notes through the canvas with a twist tie or a quick stitch with a scrap of yarn. To stay organized, you many want to store corresponding pieces together in zip-close bags.

If you want to make several of a favorite design to give as gifts or sell at bazaars, make cutting canvas easier and faster by making a master pattern. From colored canvas, cut out one of each piece required. For duplicates, place the colored canvas on top of clear canvas and cut out. If needed, secure the canvas pieces together with paper fasteners, twist ties or yarn. By using this method, you only have to count from the graphs once.

If you accidentally cut or tear a bar or two on your canvas, don't worry! Boo-boos can usually be repaired in one of several ways: heat the tip of a metal skewer and melt the canvas back together; glue torn bars with a tiny drop of craft glue, super glue or hot glue; or reinforce the torn section with a separate piece of canvas placed at the back of your work. When reinforcing with extra canvas, stitch through both thicknesses.

SUPPLIES

Yarn, canvas, needles, cutters and most other supplies needed to complete the projects in this book are available at craft and needlework stores and through mail order catalogs. Other supplies are available at fabric, hardware and discount stores.

NEEDLES & OTHER STITCHING TOOLS

Blunt-end tapestry needles are used for stitching plastic canvas. Choose a No. 16 needle for stitching 5- and 7-mesh, a No. 18 for stitching 10-mesh and a No. 24 for stitching 14-mesh canvas. A small pair of embroidery scissors for snipping yarn is handy. Try using needle-nosed jewelry pliers for pulling the needle through several thicknesses of canvas and out of tight spots too small for your hand.

STITCHING THE CANVAS

Stitching Instructions for each section are found after the Cutting Instructions. First, refer to the illustrations of basic stitches found on page 159 to familiarize yourself with the stitches used. Illustrations will be found near the graphs for pieces worked using special stitches. Follow the numbers on the tiny graph beside the illustration to make each stitch – bring your needle up from the back of the work on odd numbers and down through the front of the work on the even numbers.

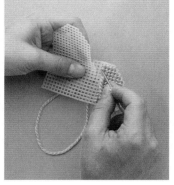

Before beginning, read the Stitching Instructions to get an overview of what you'll be doing. You'll find that some pieces are stitched using colors and stitches indicated on graphs, and for other pieces you will be given a color and stitch to use to cover the entire piece.

Cut yarn lengths between 18" [45.7cm] to 36" [91.4cm]. Thread needle; do not tie a knot in the end. Bring your needle up through the canvas from the back, leaving a short length of yarn on the wrong side of the canvas. As you begin to stitch, work over this short length of yarn. If you are beginning with Continental Stitches, leave a 1" [2.5cm] length, but if you are working longer stitches, leave a longer length.

In order for graph colors to contrast well, graph colors may not match yarn colors. For instance, a light yellow may be selected to represent the metallic cord color gold, or a light blue may represent white yarn.

When following a graph showing several colors, you may want to work all the stitches of one color at the same time. Some stitchers prefer to work with several colors at once by threading each on a separate needle and letting the yarn not being used hang on the wrong side of the work. Either way, remember that strands of yarn run across the wrong side of the work may show through the stitches from the front.

As you stitch, try to maintain an even tension on the yarn. Loose stitches will look uneven, and tight stitches will let the canvas show through. If your yarn twists as you work, you may want to let your needle and yarn hang and untwist occasionally.

When you end a section of stitching or finish a thread, weave the yarn through the back side of your last few stitches, then trim it off.

CONSTRUCTION & ASSEMBLY

After all pieces of an item needing assembly are stitched, you will find the order of assembly is listed in the Stitching Instructions and sometimes illustrated in Diagrams found with the graphs. For best results, join pieces in the order written. Refer to the Stitch Key and to the directives near the graphs for precise attachments.

FINISHING TIPS

To combat glue strings when using a hot glue gun, practice a swirling motion as you work. After placing the drop of glue on your work, lift the gun slightly and swirl to break the stream of glue, as if you were making an ice cream cone. Have a cup of water handy when gluing. For those times that you'll need to touch the glue, first dip your finger into the water just enough to dampen it. This will minimize the glue sticking to your finger, and it will cool and set the glue more quickly.

To attach beads, use a bit more glue to form a cup around the bead. If too much shows after drying, use a craft knife to trim off excess glue.

Scotchguard® or other fabric protectors may be used on your finished projects. However, avoid using a permanent marker if you plan to use a fabric protector, and be sure to remove all other markings before stitching. Fabric protectors can cause markings to bleed, staining yarn.

FOR MORE INFORMATION

Sometimes even the most experienced needlecrafters can find themselves having trouble following instructions. If you have difficulty completing your project, write to Plastic Canvas Editors, The Needlecraft Shop, 23 Old Pecan Road, Big Sandy, Texas 75755 (903) 636-4000 or (800) 259-4000, www.needlecraftshop.com.

STITCH GUIDE

Backstitch

French Knot

Rya Knot

Continental

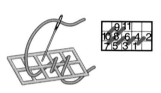

Long Over Three Bars

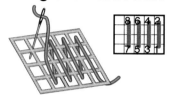

Scotch Over Three Bars

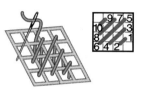

Continental Reverse

Modified Turkey Work

Smyrna Small T-Over

Cross

Overcast

Smyrna Large T-Over

Diagonal Horizontal

Plaited Rose

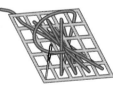

Straight

Diagonal Reverse Horizontal

Running Over Two

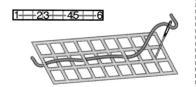

Whipstitch

PATTERN INDEX

DESIGNER INDEX